The Space Between

Creating Conscious Boundaries for Deep Connection and Authentic Alignment

Jennifer Main

For my Tribe,

past, present, and future

Contents

Part III: Live Your Calling

Introduction

Over the past decade, clients and students have more frequently asked for guidance and deeper understanding of their boundary issues, and of what could change within their lives as a result. Once I began to notice clear patterns within these issues, the importance of applying appropriate boundaries became obvious. It also became clear that to some degree, most of us are lacking in this clarity. Even when we are very healthy in one area, we may be lagging behind in others, and making the whole congruent, all aspects in harmony, is what creates a healthy life. I began to introduce elements of boundary awareness and implementation into my sessions and workshops, because I found that the boundary problems were seeping into every aspect of life. As the teachings were applied, circumstances began to change, because of the new ways in which issues were being responded to.

One of the most interesting aspects of my research into, and writing about barriers to boundaries, was how the process brought my own issues to the surface. I freely admit that I was not entirely prepared for this process when I began. As a practitioner and instructor, I historically have been able to set healthy boundaries, but I began to recognise the subtle problems that were simmering away under the surface. I delved in, hoping to learn from the experience, and I certainly did.

The goal of this book is, through sharing stories, theory, and practical application, to provide the reader with tools to overcome fear, doubt, and barriers to boundaries. The benefits of mastering the ability to choose our boundaries are worth the time and effort, because once the lessons are applied, every aspect of life is simplified. We stop fighting others and ourselves. At this very moment, we are at war: we are at war with ourselves and have been throughout our entire lives. Some of us have become masters of deception. We have convinced ourselves that everything is 'fine'. We have avoided conflict and confrontation by ignoring inner turmoil. Or, we have played an active part in the drama created along the way, in our personal and professional lives, and within ourselves. At some point we play both of these rolls, simply because it is what we have always known.

Over the course of lifetimes and generations, human beings have accepted various roles and identities. Most of these labels have served to create an opposition, making one right and another wrong. As we adopt and live these identities, we are challenged by the perception of their validity—because they are not the truth. No label can embody the complete truth of who we are. Yet we wear them, and we fight them, and we love them and hate them, accept and reject them. And the cycle of inner battle continues. What if we could end the battle? What if the war was over? Without the conflict and drama, what would change? We have the ability to make a choice: *truth or fear.*

There are a few core values that are universal; among these are *truth* and *freedom*. The presence of these values in our lives is both the problem and the solution. Truth is the constant, grounding foundation of existence, but freedom allows us to choose otherwise. Without an understanding of truth, we live in conflict because we give into illusion, which is based in fear. Fear is very simply a lack of truth. Fear is misunderstanding, confusion, an inability to move beyond belief. Freedom provides us with the ability to choose our experiences, and we often choose to believe what serves us on some level. As you read this book and consider your life, identify the areas that feel true. You will notice that they feel lighter, clearer, more grounded. And the areas that are out of alignment feel heavier, confused, and triggering. The conflict and suffering that we experience always stems from an inability to live, see, and feel the truth, what is authentic, what aligns with calling, and then bowing to the fear that we feel. Ask yourself: are you ready to set yourself free?

As we progress, I will be speaking to various levels of your *being*. As a soul, you already know everything that I write. The purpose of this book is simply to remind you of what you already know. It is common to believe that you 'forget' yourself, on the human or subconscious level. In truth, you simply fail to remember your true state of allowing and being. So the bulk of this book is for your human aspect. Part of you may resist this, as many spiritual teachers are quick to dismiss the ego, or the human experience. The teachings repeatedly instruct to forget our humanity and only focus on what is beyond. But if that is all we are meant to do, why would we choose to live?

This experience, this lifetime, is important. This life is not to be dismissed. To dismiss it is to dishonour *you*, and all that you are here to do. We are infinitely complex, an amalgamation of various aspects and vibration, and we choose to exist here and now, for this limited time, in order to learn, grow, and evolve. I hope to help you transcend your perceived limitations, and to feel more connected and at home.

Here and now, we have an opportunity to create heaven on earth. The two are intertwined, ever present, and we can embody both in this lifetime as we learn to embrace the experience, instead of fighting against all it has to offer. Most of what I share will be offered to satisfy your human mind, the ego, and the subconscious, and by resolving the confusion, to speak to you as a *soul* as well. The goal is graceful integration, and all you have to do to is allow.

The title of this book is 'The Space Between.' For you, this may address the space between you and those you love, or what you love to do. It could be the space between who you are and who you want to be, or the disconnection with your *true self*, the struggle to remember your essence. Ultimately, the purpose of the book is to guide you back to yourself, back into alignment, back to self, soul, and home.

Part I:

Understand Your Choices

Chapter 1: The First Steps

You have already begun. You have courageously taken your first steps on the Great Journey of Enlightenment, following the yellow brick road, or the road less travelled. You are broadening your horizons, reading new books, learning from master teachers, listening to your body, eating what nourishes, beginning to focus on your intuition and desires. The future looks bright and beautiful. You have more clarity of what feels good, what is aligned with your values, and are giving yourself permission to explore the possibilities. You finally feel as though you are beginning to live up to your potential.

And then, it feels as though it is slipping through your fingers; you are losing your newly found footing and foundation. Aspects within your life begin to shift and crumble, and you feel the ground beneath you open up to swallow you whole. We often begin the journey to alignment, assuming that the road to bliss is blissful, only to find that there are still bumps, detours, and difficulties along the way. A great irony of life is that we fight against the obstacles, only to find that we have been given what we asked for. We ask for growth and awareness, and are given opportunities to gain both, in the ways that we are able to learn. If we are able to grow from loving and expansive experiences, we will. But if we believe on some level that the only way to grow is through pain, suffering, or deprivation, we create these opportunities too.

At various points in our lives, we call upon ourselves to step up. We realise that we are not living our highest potential, and we know that we can do better, and be better. We strive to learn more, practice harder, and set our sights to a higher level. This added effort could be applied within our careers, our partnerships, our physical health or appearance, or with very specific skills. We could simply want to improve the time in which 5K is run, or our level of patience with our children. We may desire more honesty in our conversations, or to become a master within our career field. We consistently want to be better, look better, feel better, know better, striving to improve, and so set goals, make plans, and set the intention to learn and grow.

And this is where our suffering begins. We discover that if we want to be better, there is a corresponding sacrifice or trade. For those of us who demand more peace in our lives, we find we must let go of conflict. Conflict appears to show us how to release it. For those of us who are begging for more love, we must face all that we hate in ourselves, so that we can learn to truly love. If we want to lead, we will find our flaws first. We will see the ways that we can improve before we are able to step into a leadership role on a larger scale. We will find the ways that we judge others, dismiss them, refuse to listen, the ways we take our roles for granted, all the ways that we could misuse our status. And when we are honest with ourselves, and we learn to do better, we become better.

In order to reach the summit, we must shed all that limits you. As the great Toni Morrison tells us, 'You wanna fly, you gotta give up the shit that weighs you down'. If we really want to be the best version of ourselves, we first must face what does not align.

A few years ago, I had a wake-up call. Little things had been building; there were subtle signs, an underlying rumbling. And I ignored them. I did what a lot of people do, and assumed that it would just blow over. I avoided having conversations because I did not want to feed the drama. But the drama grew teeth. People I loved told me that they no longer loved me, in the most humiliating way. I manifested my worst fears. The pain was enough to make me doubt myself. I questioned my relationships, my ability to be a teacher or leader, my ability to make good choices. I began to doubt everything that I was doing. This was one of the most unhappy periods of my life, and also the most illuminating. Eventually I was able to step back and took a long, hard look at myself and what I had been creating. And then I got to work.

The reality is that I could have prevented the heartache. If I had addressed the small issues when they were small, I could have prevented the pain. I began to look at how the issues in my life connected and how they impacted upon one another. I realised that it all boiled down to one issue: boundaries.

What do you think of when you consider boundaries? *Boundary* is often a loaded word, saturated with emotion, old belief, and experience. So for now, I want you to let go of what you think you know about boundaries, and begin to think of them as *choices*. Setting a boundary is simply choosing an experience, interaction, feeling, the dynamics within our relationships, and the way we experience life.

First, it is important to understand the difference between a boundary and a barrier. A barrier is created from fear, an attempt to stop what we fear. We may create barriers against love, connection, our own essence, and truth, simply because we fear what would happen if we lost them. We create barriers to prevent pain and suffering that has not even occurred. A barrier is an overcompensation, an extreme reaction. Barriers are established as a reaction to a past experience, and prevent new possibilities and potential in the present and future.

A boundary is more fluid, less absolute, and is chosen when we are able to discern truth from fear, and to trust. When we get it right, relationships click, and they grow and flow. When we don't, they don't. Ultimately, a boundary is a choice. Introducing a boundary is simply choosing an experience, on purpose.

We all desire more freedom in our lives, on a deep, soul level. We may also be afraid of what that could mean, or the impact it would have, but as eternal beings, we know limitless freedom and we feel homesick for it. When we begin to choose our boundaries, we begin to choose the course of our lives. On some level, we are always choosing, but when we begin to make the decision conscious, to choose on purpose, our life experience moves into another level of creation and awareness. Instead of going through the motions, or simply opting for what we have always done, we begin to choose our behaviour, our mood, how we feel, the ways we react, and what we do. When we soften our barriers and apply boundaries, our lives shift to align with our deeper sense of self.

Can you remember life as a child, your earliest years? What you recall are possibly just hazy moments and vague sensations, but the memories are there. We are born with inherited traits and memories, but beyond them is our connection to *ourselves*. We arrived with fresh memory, of existence before this life. We were born with purpose and calling, and are still strongly connected to that beautiful, ethereal soul energy, our essence. But over years of life on this planet, within this plane, that connection can seem to dull. We forgot our miracles only to focus on the more earthly occurrences—because we want to belong. We want to connect with other human beings, and in order to do this, we conform to what is expected.

This pattern is the same for all of us. But once we become conscious of the increasing space between who we are and who we believe we are, we can begin to close the gap, and be wholly aligned.

Awakening

Most spiritual teachers will tell us that enlightenment is the goal for each of us. In reality, we are already enlightened souls, attempting to connect and share with the rest of existence. This world provides a platform for sensation, expression, an opportunity to find the best options for each of us. When you look at your past, are you able to recognise times when you were more awake or aware? As children, we were more aware of the present moment, of what we were doing, simply *being*. As we age, our brain naturally moves into beta brainwaves, the conscious mind, and as we move more into the more logical mind, we feel less present, less grounded, less aware of the whole picture.

I know this from my own experience—I can see how my perception changed through my teenage and adult years. I began to follow the opinions of others, because I felt unsure when making a decision. In many ways, I was on auto-pilot, just doing what I thought I was supposed to do. This continued until I began to see the patterns and understand that I was choosing, not from an awareness, but out of habit. I worked far too many hours, because that is what members of my family had always done. I entered into the field of social work, because that is what my parents did. I learned from these experiences and loved many aspects of the work, but I believe that my life would have felt more aligned, a better fit, if I had been more awake and aware. Once I began to see the patterns and understand the cause and effect, I was able to change.

Once we become aware of the patterns that are simply habit, that do not serve, we are then able to create change. The beginning of our awakening is an exercise in reflection, awareness, and beginning to truly understand the link between cause and effect. It is in accepting responsibility for ourselves, for our circumstances that we choose the change we wish to experience in our lives. Awakening is the courageous choice. Sleeping is the easy option. We can be inspired by choosing *more than* average, more than acceptable. The awakening process is not the easy way, but it is the most fulfilling.

You are a Creator

What we focus on, and feel, shows up in our lives, and you can perceive the world around you as a mirror to what you are experiencing within. This world is miraculous, in that everything around us can teach us something about ourselves. Manifesting teachers state that we are magnets, receiving what we think about, and this is true to a degree. I once manifested free fudge from a stranger on the street because I spoke to my friends about how much I wanted some. But I also know that just because you talk about something does not necessarily mean that object will appear.

Think of yourself as the creator of your life. There are multiple facets of yourself that are directing the action at any point. On one level, your soul is running the show, lining up the big, meaningful events for you. But your subconscious plays a massive role in your day to day. Your subconscious keeps track of your doubts and fears, and the pain that you have experienced. Once the pain hits a tipping point, it has to be dealt with, and we begin to see this in our bodies, relationships, synchronicity, and major life events.

We know that stress has a physical effect on the body. Extreme or prolonged stress effects blood pressure, digestion, energy levels, and once the stress becomes more than the body can handle, the body begins to shut down, and to shut us down. The same happens with emotion. If we are holding anger, and allowing it to grow or fester, it can affect the physical body, in an attempt to motivate a change. Our anger attracts more situations to be angry, so that it builds to a point that we can no longer ignore. We are not attracting like for like simply because we are magnets. We will attract whatever will allow us to see that there is another way of *being*.

Why do you think that others are mean to you, belittle you, ignore or dismiss you? How others abuse us is how we abuse ourselves. All of the ways in which the world is unfair represents the ways that we sell ourselves short, deny ourselves happiness, or fear growth. What triggers you about your relationships? Your job? Your friendships? Your place in the world? What are you trying to learn about your own relationship with yourself through these interactions? The answers that we are looking for in the world around us can always be found within. When we feel angry or sad because of another, when we resent our circumstances, we are invited to understand a deeper aspect of ourselves. We will always create in our outer world a focus to bring us back inside. You are not a magnet, drawing like for like. You are a creator, manifesting what will facilitate meaningful growth.

Chapter 2: Becoming Conscious

Every human being has a conscious mind and a subconscious mind. The conscious mind is aware of the surface, but not always the depths. Within our conscious state, we are aware of reading these words, hearing sounds from the busy street outside, feeling the texture of clothing touching skin, or the temperature of the room. This awareness influences the thoughts that are a part of our minute to minute experience that we witness as our daily life. These are the thoughts, feelings, and sensations that we have a conscious awareness of focusing on, noticing, and remembering, throughout the day. The conscious mind is easy to monitor, simply because we are aware of what we are thinking or focused upon.

As we begin to sink below the surface, we meet the subconscious, a much deeper part of ourselves. Along with the conscious awareness as you read, there may also be a triggering of a memory of a childhood friend, or of an interaction from last month, feelings of nostalgia, or a change in your emotional state. Our subconscious is more inclusive, more complete story, and the culmination of past experiences, identity, ego, and the beliefs and feelings that influence our conscious mind. Whether we are aware or not, we are always responding to our subconscious self. Our feelings and emotions, memories, our identity and beliefs are always accessible, and playing a part in each moment.

Meditation, inner reflection, mindful stillness, are all ways to become more aware of our deeper levels. As we delve within, we connect with all that is occurring and unfolding within the body.

Anything that we do to connect with how we feel will take us deeper. Taking the time to connect with various parts of the body, noticing how we feel, any sensations or awareness, or simply nurturing ourselves will do the same. Exercise, eating, sex, and anything that allows us to be present, feeling grounded and present in the current moment, brings us back to our body and helps us reconnect.

To varying degrees, we avoid connecting with the subconscious in a meaningful way. There is fear in facing the past, old emotion, and in the possibility of experiencing the pain of a memory over and over again. The subconscious is where we hold our fears, our pain and suffering, memory of past experiences of failure, regret, and resentments. We often choose to avoid discomfort, to ignore as much as possible, and continue to do so until it becomes too painful to avoid. But if we attempt to avoid suffering over long periods of time, it often takes a crisis of some sort to get our attention, to address the depths. Addiction, health scares, near death experiences, and prolonged suffering are often the motivation for change. We often hear about at addict having to hit rock bottom, or a person receiving a diagnosis proving that there is a problem, in order to choose change.

In order for change to occur, we first must recognise what is causing the problem and why. Our belief systems are complex, dynamic, ever changing, responding to each interaction and circumstance. When we attempt to simplify the complex, to keep it from overwhelming, the results are often short-sighted, limited decisions. Our subconscious holds memory as a point of reference, so that we do not repeat mistakes. But because it first focuses on what it believes to be important, we often make decisions without being aware of the bigger picture. Our brain does something called thin slicing, which gives it an incredible ability to make an accurate judgement with only a few seconds to take in information. This ability is perfect for a quick assessment, but possibly not when deciding to create bigger changes in our lives. Our subconscious has access to nearly infinite information, from our lifetime, our ancestors, and from the collective consciousness. Learning to tap into the useful information will allow us to find a solution to anything. But the key, of course, is choosing the option that is most true, and best applies.

A study was conducted years ago, with a group of children. Each child was given a marshmallow, and told that if he or she could wait until the researcher came back, two would be given. Once the researcher left the room, the children were watched, to see if they were able to apply the concept of delayed gratification, which would enable them to have more of what they wanted if they simply waited. Some children immediately ate the marshmallow. Some children tried desperately to distract themselves, sit on their hands, and keep themselves from eating the single marshmallow. And some found it easy to wait and to be rewarded for their patience.

How often do we eat a meal that we know our bodies will not appreciate, that will make us feel heavy or tired, or that we will feel guilty about soon after? How often do we choose to watch television instead of going for a walk, when we know that the exercise would energise us, and we would feel happier with ourselves? Most of us will automatically choose what feels good *now*, instead of choosing what would actually serve us in the long term. So you can see why making a change can take time and effort. Most people do not change overnight, and it often takes time, motivation, or fear to trigger meaningful change. But we can begin to understand ourselves, to listen to our bodies, and nourish ourselves in ways that allow us to be more conscious and aware of our deeper selves.

Chapter 3: Ego & Identity

We love to hate the *ego*, the source of all pain and suffering, the worst of humanity, the saboteur. Or is it? The ego has been given many names, most of which are insulting and full of fear, because we associate the ego with the worst of us: the jealousy, competition, selfishness, aggressive aspects that motivate us to act in shameful ways. We are taught in many modalities and philosophies to deny the ego, to kill it. But as a human being, we will always have an ego; it is an integral part of the human experience. When we fight against the ego, we fight against ourselves. How many rounds have you already fought?

What is essential to appreciate is that the ego is part of what makes us unique in this lifetime. Our personality, our sense of humour, all of the quirks and nuances that we embrace within us are part of the ego. Our passions and pleasures are an aspect of ego. Our enjoyment of horror movies, the push to compete, or win a race, all of the little guilty pleasures, of watching silly movies, discussing comic books with our friends, learning everything we can about the actor we admire, the fascination with our favourite authors, are all part of the ego. If we fight, dismiss, or kill the ego as we have been instructed, what would our lives look like? They would be less colourful, less fun, incomplete. The key to loving the *self* is to learn to love the ego. Give up the battle, and accept it for what it is. We do not have to give into tendencies, thoughts, or beliefs that are less than kind. Once we become conscious of the ego's workings, we can then decide what to act on, what to love, and what to release. We get to choose the lighter, higher aspects of any part of us, and express our human selves through the filter of the ego.

The beauty of the ego is that it provides a reference point to look deeper within. If your hobby is birdwatching, you can use this as a reference point for learning more about yourself. You may love watching birds because you value calm, or your admire their freedom, or maybe you appreciate colour or grace. If you love horror movies, maybe you value excitement and adventure, or like to see the world from multiple perspectives. You can always ask yourself why you choose to express yourself through the filters in specific ways, and use the ego to teach you more about your spirit.

A major part of the ego is created by identity. As infinite beings, we are limitless, label-less, and beyond defining. As human beings, we spend our entire lives trying to identify who we are. We are hardwired to learn through comparison, contrast, cause and effect. We learn through trial and error, and carry these memories throughout life, even in our DNA.

Scientists are now able to show that memory is shared and handed down through DNA. Newly hatched baby birds will immediately run for cover if they see a shadow of a hawk flying overhead. But if the same shadow is moving backwards, they will ignore it. The chicks know on a primal level what is a threat and what is not.

We can also look at our own family lines and recognise qualities that we inherited from previous generations. Your great grandmother may have understood how to grow herbs or crops, and you can tap into this knowledge, stored within your cells, and understand how to grow your own. You may also know on some level to avoid certain plants because an ancestor became ill from coming into contact with the same plant generations ago.

Our subconscious keeps record of these experiences as a short cut to learning. This keeps us from having to repeat the same mistakes that our ancestors made, or that we made as a child. Do you remember burning yourself on the stove, cutting or injuring yourself, and then knowing to avoid the same behaviour? Memory, and understanding of cause and effect enable us to live and learn. We also learn that as we experience life, we identify what is enjoyable and what is not. We learn that we prefer one type of food over the other, so one type is judged to be good, and the other not. We learn to judge and ultimately reject what we do not prefer to experience. This is not necessarily wrong, but when our judgments become fixed and we are unable to alter or question them, this can create barriers to new experiences and growth.

Inevitably, we begin to label. We label other people, other countries, cultures, religions, experiences. We label because we want to understand, so that we can communicate our experiences with others. We believe that we can understand something once it has a label, and it makes us feel more comfortable, more connected with those who resonate, or who 'speak the same language'. And often, we feel uncomfortable when something or someone refuses to fit within the labels, the rebels, with non-conformists, or anyone who refuses to fit the status quo. On some level, we feel a need to understand, so that we do not fear the unknown.

We also affix labels so that we can understand ourselves. We naturally want to fit in with a community or tribe, and so we accept our own labels to match others. We crave a sense of home, belonging, and acceptance. But as we develop and evolve, we outgrow various aspects of that particular community and expand beyond. Through evolution, we begin to recognise that the labels that were previously worn now feel limiting and small. We then reject and rebel against the identity that we searched for.

Ultimately, the exercise in understanding who we are beyond words, labels, language, provides an opportunity to recognise ourselves as timeless beings in a time-bound existence, the infinite in a finite space. We accept and reject so that we can understand how to transcend, and live without them.

Chapter 4: Judgement, Conflict & Fear

As we begin to judge, conflict plays its part in our relationships, with others and ourselves. We have infinite opportunities every day to sense, feel, consider, compare, and decide. Contrast and polarity gives way to an understanding of the options on offer, and ultimately a choice in what aligns. Once we begin to identify the difference between what we do or do not want, we can choose a response.

The dominant tendency is to judge and label the undesirable as *bad* or *wrong*. And we then build barriers, a purely protective behaviour. We want to protect ourselves from what we judge to be 'wrong'. On one level, we do this simply to avoid feeling uncomfortable, upset, or worse, but we also do this so that we do not become 'bad'. How often do we reject a person, or their behaviour, because we do not want to act in the same way? How often to we push another away because we do not want to be affected by their words or energy?

We all do this. We avoid negative people because we do not want to be pulled down with them. We cut people out of our lives who could damage our reputation, image, or how the world views us. We judge and reject those who are cheaters, liars, addicts, violent, criminals, but we also do this with each of the 'lesser evils'.

I grew up in the southeast of the United States, and in the South, manners are almost mandatory, a way of life. We open the doors for others, say 'Yes ma'am' and 'Yes sir', we bless everyone who sneezes. I know that I have a slightly nostalgic view of my childhood, as we all do, and have romanticised just how kind people are, based on the ability to be polite. But part of me deeply values those who outwardly show respect and kindness to others in my community. As a result, I used to judge rudeness harshly. I would become frustrated with people who did not show gratitude, who ignored another's personal space, who smoked in public, or anything that I judged to be disrespectful behaviour. I am sure that I made snap judgements over the years against kind and caring individuals, who happened to show one rude habit.

When I looked more deeply into the motivation behind this, I realised that I was holding onto resentment towards disrespectful people because I was afraid that I could be like them. On some level, I believed that if I accepted others wholly, I would accept myself wholly, and would become a bad person. The resentment was keeping me in check. The harsh judgement helped me remember that being rude was 'bad', and that I had to judge, to keep from becoming rude myself. I know this sounds extreme, but this is what we do. When you consider what you hate or resent, ask yourself what you are protecting yourself from.

Using Fear as a Teacher

We spend our lives being defined by family, a job, our culture, religion, nationality, and none of these labels can come close to showing us the truth of ourselves. Our labels give us a point of reference, to help us to know where we might fit in, but *beyond* our labels is where the full picture lies. As we begin to reconnect with ourselves, we begin to gain more clarity about who we really are. As we search and turn inward to our fears, we begin unearthing the mystery within. Fear is a lack of truth, clarity, or alignment within, and we can look to our fears to show us where we are most confused, and also most able to reconnect.

Consider the aspect of your life that causes the most stress. The stress is caused by an inner conflict, which stems from a knowing on a higher level of what aligns, and a lack of understanding on another. Your inner conflict will grow until it is resolved. When you harbour a conflict within, it begins to show up in your life in various ways. It usually starts small, a little hiccup in a plan, annoyance, irritation. And as you ignore it, or remain less conscious of the issue, it grows, and begins to create drama. Facing the drama in your life can have the biggest impact, when you decide to resolve the conflict.

We, as human beings, are complex, with layers of emotion, beliefs, thoughts, energy. The drama that we create is the consequence of a deeper discord; it is the symptom. We routinely attempt to treat the symptom without addressing the root cause, like continuously taking medication to ease back pain, instead of seeing the true source of the pain. Even though we are complex, everything is connected. I have clients who come to me with major issues in a few different areas of their lives, and each issue seems wholly unrelated to the next. If there is drama in a person's relationship with a partner, a problem with physical health, fear of applying for a new job, and difficulty paying off debt, the chances are high that they are all connected in some way. If the client had addressed the root issue in the beginning, when it was just a small annoyance towards the partner, it could have been resolved then, but ignoring the issue when it was small meant that it spread to other areas, manifesting in new ways, to gain some attention. So although you may feel overwhelmed by the problems in your life, the solution may be much simpler than you think.

After years of working through issues with my clients, I begin to see regular patterns in the beliefs and emotions that helped to create them. Belief systems are important to address, because they influence our thinking, our decisions, and ultimately our behaviour. But if we can get down below them, we get back to ourselves. As we dig down into fear, we face what we have been denying or fighting to forget for decades. Underneath all of that fear is our essence, the memory of who we are, and the lightness of that truth. When we feel disconnected from our source or soul, we can use fear as a way to remember.

Motivation or Inspiration?

When you think back to the biggest changes in your life, were they *motivated* by fear, or were they *inspired* by something within? There is a big difference between motivation and inspiration, producing very different results. Motivation is always triggered by something external to ourselves. We are motivated to react to someone else. Students can study longer hours because they want to prevent conflict with their parents. Athletes can train harder because they are determined to defeat their competitors. We can all look back at our lives and see when we have chosen to react to a situation out of fear.

When I first started my own business, I was a total novice and had very little idea of how to promote myself or connect with new clients. Seeing others promote themselves triggered a lot within me. I discovered that I felt jealous and competitive, which I had little previous experience with. I began to react in ways that were not in alignment with my integrity. It did motivate me to speak to others about my practice, but the energy behind the actions did not feel good. I learned at that point to identify the difference between motivation and inspiration, and how to choose change based on my virtues, not my vices.

Inspiration comes from within, and we choose to act or behave in alignment with our greater aspects. Inspired action is the result of choosing to live in alignment with the best within. Through inspiration, a student will study for the sake of learning, for the love of the process, and to be the best he can possibly be. A business owner will market herself because she knows that this is a way to help more people, to provide a service that she loves. Inspired action invites grace into the journey.

Consider what you do because you are afraid of being judged if you are caught doing it, and what you are proud to do, without needing to be prompted to do so. Once we begin to connect with the feeling of inspiration, and make choices based a feeling of alignment, instead of fear, we really begin to create inspired change. And the more we do this, the more momentum builds, along with our confidence, our sense of clarity and purpose, and the feeling of freedom. And as this grows, so do we. Move beyond the judgement and fear, and be inspired by the life you choose to live.

Chapter 5: Embracing Emotion

There are many modalities and philosophies that focus on the impact of belief systems upon our health, wellbeing, and harmony, because our belief systems play an important role in shaping our lives. But I also believe that it is emotion, how we feel, that truly shapes our beliefs. I spent years helping people to identify subconscious beliefs, but ultimately, it all came back to one question: How does this make you feel? We hold onto thinking and patterns of habit that we believe will make us *feel* better, in one way, or another. The desire to feel better motivates everything that we do.

Think back to the last time you became aware of thoughts which made you uncomfortable, that caused you to feel heavy or low. What was your response? Did you delve within, to identify what you were experiencing? Did you question where the beliefs originated? Did you locate the feeling within your body and gain clarity on the mix of emotions you were holding? Or did you eat something, drink something, organise your sock drawer, or turn on the television? Did you avoid the issue and find something to distract you from the experience? Most of us have a built-in ability to avoid discomfort if at all possible. Once it builds to a higher level of pain and suffering, we deal with it, but if we can simply switch the focus and 'forget' the pain, we will.

The reality is that simply shifting focus does not solve the problem. The discomfort will remain within until we face it and understand. But if we believe that the avoidance will make us feel better, even temporarily, the we will choose, on a subconscious level, to create barriers and avoid. But what is underneath the avoidance? When we slip below the disconnection, we connect with the pain. If we are on the path to peace, we know that we first must address the conflict, to find our way. Inevitably we fight against ourselves, our subconscious mind, to address what is necessary. But what if we could address the pain without it being a painful experience?

Imagine connecting with your most painful memory. Part of you will fight even considering this. That part of you questions, making you doubt the benefit of connecting with the suffering. But what if you could connect with the memory without the pain that you associate it with? Again, pain and suffering is simply a result of a disconnection with truth. If this is a childhood memory, you will likely have some confusion around the memory, because as children we have a more limited perspective of what is happening in the physical world. But what if you could connect with the memory, but also see the bigger picture?

What if you could see and understand the perspective of the other person or people involved, or even the country or culture, if that applies? What if you could see the pain that was motivating him to speak to you in that way? What if you could understand the suffering that she had endured, that was influencing her behaviour towards you? What would change? The pain could begin to soften. The heavy energy around the emotion would begin to lighten, and you would find that your suffering would begin to resolve. But this takes effort. Introspection requires a real desire to find the truth within any interaction, without relying on blame to make us feel better, to relieve our pain. It is not the easy path, and it requires us to release identities that we have held onto, often for decades. Delving into the emotion within is an act of courage. Are you ready to be courageous?

The Spectrum of Emotion

Human emotion is experienced in a complex spectrum. We never experience only one at a time; there is always a mixture, a cocktail of feelings that we work diligently to identify. The sensitive souls find it overwhelming. The intensity, the mixture, the complicated layers and sensations make us feel confused and overwhelmed, or that it is too much to handle.

As a child, I was always sensitive. I could feel other people's pain or discomfort, I could feel if they were angry or sad, and I could feel what they thought of me. I could feel it all, and as a child, it was difficult to understand. I have recognised over the years that emotion itself seemed to be overwhelming. It did not matter if the feelings were good or bad, if it felt strong, then it was simply too much for me to handle.

Even with opportunities to have fun, birthday parties, time with my friends, holidays with my family, I struggled to cope with my feelings. As my excitement grew, I would begin to feel discomfort, overwhelm, and then pain, and the fun would be sabotaged before the joy became too much to cope with. I think that on some level I believed that fun and excitement would kill me. Part of me would try to push the feeling away because it felt as though I would suffocate. I was rejecting the fun that I had asked for, because I simply did not know how to process what was happening on an emotional or physical level. The subconscious is not logical. It wants to keep us alive, and so if an experience or feeling is associated with pain or danger, it will do what it can to keep us from it.

On one level, we may believe that avoiding suffering lessens our perception of it, but whatever we push away impacts us on multiple levels. I have worked with hundreds of clients who have gone through periods of depression. The common complaint is less about any sadness or pain experienced, and more around a lack of positive feelings, or a lack of a contrast in emotion. They have gone through periods when life was not unbearable, but it certainly was not good.

We are equipped with a vast spectrum of emotion. They are complex, often times difficult to differentiate, and confusing, because we never experience just one at a time. When we become overwhelmed with emotion, confused by our feelings, or simply stuck in the densest end of the spectrum, we begin to push away. As we push away emotion, we disconnect not only from the negative, but from the positive as well. As we attempt to save ourselves from feeling pain, much of our suffering comes about as the result of trying to avoid the suffering.

Oftentimes, the pain comes from a misunderstanding, lack of communication, or avoiding a problem before it grows beyond what is manageable. This applies to our emotional health as well.

We may be holding onto the pain of rejection from childhood, feeling that our family members ignored or even neglected us. The truth may be that they had to work more because of financial issues, or were simply unable to show love or affection. Our perception of rejection and pain is felt deeper and does more damage than it would if we were able to see the big picture, or have the highest perspective of the dynamics at play. I am not in any way dismissing any suffering at any stage of life, as it shapes our lives, for better or worse. But when we begin to peel back the layers of avoidance, old emotion, limited perception and beliefs, we begin to see the higher truth, and learn to appreciate these experiences for what they really were, instead of judging them for what they were lacking.

What if you could see your mother as the complex being that she is, instead of seeing the ways that she failed you in your childhood? What if you could accept your father for what he was able to share, instead of feeling neglected or denied because of what he could not? Could we love our siblings more if we were able to let go of the conflict and competition of our childhood? How would our lives change if we let go of our perception, and accepted the bigger picture instead?

When we begin to evaluate our emotions in a similar way, we can understand why we rejected a large portion of them over the course of many years, especially as we struggle with the most uncomfortable. I know that I spent decades avoiding feeling angry, because I did not know how to cope with the feeling. On some level, I was afraid that it would consume me, or destroy what I had worked so hard to achieve. We can refuse to acknowledge that we may resent people in our lives, especially when we resent the ones that we also love the most. On deep levels we can hate co-workers, resent our peers, feel angry at our partner, feel jealous of friends and those in our communities. As long as we judge these feelings, we prevent ourselves from understanding why we feel them, and from being able to do something about it.

Be honest with yourself for just a moment. When you think about your relationship with your feelings, how healthy does it feel? When you feel anger rising within, do you feel guilty, do you push it back down, or do you allow yourself to feel it? What is your response to your most uncomfortable feelings? As long as you reject the experience of emotion, you reject the opportunity to be fully human, and to live as a whole and integrated being. And right now, you have the opportunity to experience the joy that comes from being alive. You are being invited to experience it all, every facet of life, and until you can do so without judging, rejecting, or avoiding, you will continue to repeat this pattern.

We all dissociate from ourselves to a degree, some much more than others. Until we are courageous enough to connect with *all* of our feelings, our experience will be limited, dulled, less vibrant and less magical. Which emotions are you willing to reconnect with, which memories are you ready to understand, in order to recreate alignment within?

Striving for the Extreme

When we are uncomfortable with, or refuse to connect with emotion, we create barriers to feeling. The desire to feel good, alongside the barriers to feel, create an inner conflict that can begin to manifest in our lives. Conflict arises as we judge, resent, and create barriers, and on some level, we also know that this way of thinking, or seeing the world, is not right for us. The barriers are an overcompensation, where the pendulum has swung too far to one side. As that pendulum swings within, the extremes pull at you, creating momentum for more contrast in your life. The contrast is not necessarily negative, but if you are feeling pulled apart, then the extremes are a good place to focus.

As you create extreme experiences, a few things can happen. The first is that you truly *feel*. Numbness, over a period of time, makes us believe that feeling *anything* might be a relief. I used to read Shakespeare's tragedies just so I could cry. Feeling sadness was better than feeling nothing. The truth is that I was not void of feeling, but I was so confused by my emotions that I needed to feel the extreme in order to identify or label the experience. The middle, or less extreme, was less defined, less distinguishable, and so I needed the more extreme to identify the emotion.

Those who are skydivers, extreme snowboarders, or anyone willing to throw themselves into extreme sports, may be attempting the same. The adrenaline creates a sense of feeling more alive, the danger focuses the mind and senses, to feel clearer than the past months or years. And after the jump, the pendulum begins to swing again, to find the next high.

The extremes are not wrong, and can be an incredible part of life, worth experiencing in ways that align with us. But if we are always chasing the high of an extreme, considering alternatives is a healthy idea. The alternative to chasing extremes is to consider our desired feelings and outcomes, and how we can create, on a daily basis, what would fulfil that sense of being alive or thriving. Imagine the pendulum slowing, the arc smaller, and the feeling that brings. It feels more centered, less erratic, more graceful. Grace does not exclude adventure and excitement. Grace is not boring or lacking in energy. Imagine the experience of a ballerina. Her body is powerful and precise, her movements are fluid and light, and each movement appears to be effortless. She has concentrated the power and precision, and channeled her energy into graceful movement, and we can do the same. Instead of erratic flailing, we can be centered, focused, and feel totally alive and free.

Chapter 6: Learning Your Language

Communication is such a complex concept, that most of us fall short in fully understanding or applying it. In some ways communicating is effortless, in that we are always naturally communicating with the world around us. On a subconscious level, we are sharing our thoughts, beliefs, emotions with others, expressing this through body language, facial expression, and various responses, conscious and unconscious. We do this whether we are aware of the process or not, and this is often the dominant aspect of any problem.

The first step in communicating effectively is to identify what we actually want to communicate. When we ourselves are a mystery, it becomes easy to see why we struggle with this. Aspects of ourselves may be a total enigma, dark and unclear, and when we begin to dip into these parts, communication also becomes unclear. We often delve into unknown areas of ourselves, without knowing that we are entering a void in understanding, and then feel uncomfortable or lost in our train of thought, words, or the way in which we want to be received. The more we cultivate acknowledgement and understanding within ourselves, and what we wish to express, the clearer our communication will be.

The next hindrance comes when we begin to express the hidden aspects of ourselves, which we are more aware of, but uncomfortable with. Speaking is often very much a logical process, and when we discuss straightforward information, our brains do their jobs very well. When we begin to introduce emotion and feeling into the conversation, the process begins to tilt. We often fight emotion, because it takes us out of the perceived clarity of logic, and down into the heart, gut, or elsewhere within the body, where logic cannot rule. We often hear advice to 'get out of our head and into our heart.' I believe that we can meet in the middle and learn to express every aspect of ourselves. How would your communication change if you allowed your head and heart to meet, expressing the harmony between the two? How many barriers have you built against the two meeting? There is always a place for logic and common sense, when it is applied to expressing the deeper aspects of ourselves, the true you.

There is an art to deep and true expression—we are learning as we go. The best communicators are not those who are solely logical or grounded, but those who understand the language of *self*. When we stop fighting against aspects of our inner being, we hear the symphony of mind, body, and soul. The symphony is our true language, our most honest expression, and it can only be heard when we embrace the beauty of it all.

Express Yourself

When we begin to understand our emotional overwhelm, a lot of confusion in our lives suddenly begins to make sense. If we are afraid to experience emotion in a healthy way, it begins to influence our thoughts, words, expression, and behaviour. The ignored or repressed emotion begins to seep out, to be expressed in ways that we would not consciously choose.

First, consider anger. What does anger feel like to you? If it had a colour or shape, how would it appear? If you could identify anger within your body, where would it be? We have a few unhealthy options in dealing with emotion. We can refuse to connect with it, and refuse to deal with it. Or spend time and energy running away from it, afraid that it will control us. Or we can allow the anger to consume us, lashing out at the people around us.

Most of us are extremely uncomfortable with feeling angry. Anger is unpleasant to experience, and we often judge ourselves for feeling angry. Anger is a natural human response, but we believe that we should not experience it, because we judge angry people. We might think that they are impatient, harsh, out of control, and try our best to keep ourselves from being angry. But we do not get to exempt ourselves from the human condition, from the spectrum emotion. We can learn to understand it, and learn to experience our emotions without fearing that they will control us.

When we feel angry, we have an opportunity to learn about ourselves, to practice choosing our response. I spent most of my life avoiding anger. I was afraid of confrontation and would avoid any potential conflict as long as possible. Unresolved issues would build until I got so angry that I could no longer hold back. These are the moments that I look back on and wish I had responded differently. I regretted waiting until I felt that I had to fight. On some level, I knew that an uncomfortable or painful exchange was possible, which is why I avoided conversation. I would imagine that anger was like a dragon, and that if I released it, it would burn down my world, destroy my relationships, and my loved ones would disappear. So the fire would burn within me instead.

In reality I was not 'saving' anyone else, but I was harming myself. I had to learn how to express myself in a way that was not abusive, or motivated by fear. I simply had to change my relationship with anger, and learn what anger was trying to tell me. If I had listened sooner, I would have learned more about communication and expression, how to say no and set a healthy boundary, how to understand others who were struggling with the same. Eventually, I learned patience, and how to accept others who might be easy to judge instead.

Our emotions can be our greatest allies, our best teachers, but we must first surrender to the experience of feeling, in order to understand them. Which emotions do you feel the most resistance towards? Sadness, grief, frustration, anxiety? As you consider the options, notice how you feel. As the discomfort sets in, ask yourself what you could say or do that would release the feeling. The emotions that you most fear are the ones that could be teaching you your greatest lessons, if you can listen. Get comfortable with being a little uncomfortable, and allow yourself to learn. Allow yourself to identify the risk, and find your edge - your greatest opportunities for healing and growth are on the other side.

Chapter 7: Boundaries

When we first begin to think about boundaries, fear or discomfort is usually triggered. We often associate creating a boundary with people who are a little parasitical, who suck us dry, with those we judge to be threatening, or those who we simply do not trust. This is an aspect of understanding and applying boundaries, but it is a small part of the picture. A boundary is a choice, and we often begin to learn and grow through choosing what we do not want.

Recently, I listened to a writer named Jeff Goins make the statement, 'Pick a fight', and I was surprised at my reaction. In the past I had heard that statement as encouragement to go out and pick a fight, to be aggressive, to force my beliefs upon others. But what he was actually saying was to pick a fight, pick a battle, pick something worth talking about, something that inspires. His message was to join the conversation, not try to control it.

I believe that many people think of setting boundaries as having to pick a fight, be aggressive, to fight for what we want. I do not believe that fighting solves anything, and will never tell you to fight with others, or with the world, to get what you want. But I will encourage you to discover what is worth a conversation, a change in your own thoughts and actions, and a shift in your life.

Barriers to Boundaries

Our greatest barriers to creating boundaries are our own fears. Fear can feel powerful, tangible, real, but is never what it seems to be. The fear we feel can seems to be more real than the love or peace that also resides within us. Because of its perceived power, we often listen to fear before we consider the alternative.

Our subconscious works hard to keep us alive, and will hold onto fear to prevent us from taking a risk. This is useful from a survival point of view, but not when our desire is to expand beyond survival and into a thriving existence. As a physical being with an ancient limbic system, a reptile brain, and instincts that link back millions of years, we are wired to pay attention to fear, to increase our chances of survival. When you think about fear, where do you feel it in your body? What aspects of your life scare you the most? What are you most afraid to do, or to change in your life?

Nature is inherently evolutionary, and our natural path follows the flow of evolution. Those who refuse to accept change as a part of life are fighting existence itself. And we are not here to stay the same, to stick with the same old beliefs and behaviour, or to suffer with our fear. We are here not only to survive, but to thrive. But often, when faced with an opportunity or decision, the default is to follow the fear. We imagine the worst possible outcome, a backlash, judgment and reaction from those around us, and we hesitate. Instead of feeling excited about the trip we were invited to join, we see the plane crash, fights with our friends, the money that will be spent. We shoot down opportunities before we really consider the growth they could provide.

When we heed fear, it feels real, and often overpowering. But when you really look at fear, and examine what stopped you in the past, did the fearful stories really come true? Obviously, yes, there are times when our fears do manifest, but it is so very rare for it to happen to the degree we imagine. So why do we listen to fear? Other than our survival instinct, our fear can serve a greater purpose. Fear can highlight the areas of our lives where we are out of alignment, lacking truth and clarity. Whenever we try something new, push beyond our comfort zone, our subconscious will trigger fear. If our primitive brain cannot predict what will happen the first time we eat sushi, sing in public, or drive a car, it will warn us that it is dangerous. The key is to change the relationship with fear.

What if we could recognise our fear towards surfing, but also be aware that the fear indicates that we are doing something new, and congratulate ourselves for doing it anyway? What if we could embrace that fear as a sign that we are evolving, learning something new, and changing our life experience, instead of seeing it as a signal to turn away?

Just because we cannot totally predict every outcome, it does not mean that we should not welcome a new experience. If we logically knew everything that would happen to us, we would not do much of anything. We would be bored, and our confidence would be non-existent, because we would lack the experiences to help us to build it. Facing fear and choosing to act in spite of it is what successful, well-rounded, grounded people do. It is a choice that is made daily, despite what fear is saying.

Moving Beyond Your Comfort Zone

As you begin to change your relationship with fear, you begin to open to the possibility of embracing all that can set you free. Freedom is a such a vast concept, encompassing every possible option, every possible thought or action. We ask for freedom on a regular basis, and then realise that we must first clear the barriers, which can create disorder, in one area or another. I remember attempting to understand the vastness of the universe in my middle school science class. It gave me a headache, and I am pretty sure that I started to panic on a subconscious level. When we begin to consider the vast nature of freedom, of infinite choice, we can understand how a person may begin to question whether they actually want the freedom the once begged for, or even demanded. Having freedom allows opportunity to choose our experiences, but when choosing is difficult, we may resist available options. Our indecision or resistance to choose may be all that is keeping us from what we desire.

When you imagine having total freedom in your life, how do you feel? Without barriers, nothing to get in your way, no excuses, nothing to blame, no hindrance, are you sure you still want it? On a conscious level, you may believe that the choice is obvious, of course you want freedom. But when you really *feel* into the idea, there may be resistance to the possibility. Notice what is getting in the way: is it indecision? How do you respond when faced with a decision? When we ask for freedom, indecision may be our biggest hindrance, stemming from confusion and avoidance. When there is a conflict in making a decision, we can either choose to resolve the conflict, or avoid it. However, avoidance simply prolongs the discomfort of self-imposed stagnation.

Indecision can also stem from anticipating regret. We are often afraid of making the wrong choice, and then regretting the choice in the future. We regret our decisions before we have even made them! We have been taught to choose based on logic, not our intuition or gut feeling. How often do we choose what makes the most sense, only to find that life unfolds in another way? Then we judge ourselves, believing that we got it wrong, and that we should have known better.

At our worst moments, many of us wait until we get to the point of being so uncomfortable that we have to make a choice. We have to get sick and tired of hearing our inner voice debating, telling us what to do, feeling the inner conflict of justification and excuses. Deep down, we know that there is a better way, but struggle to change with grace. We attempt to change in stages, but once we lose momentum, we can feel as though we are floating adrift. And then we try to *make* things happen. In those moments I have tried all of the manifesting 'tricks' that I know of. But I then recognise that my excuses and indecision are holding sway over me, and I let them go. There will always be infinite reasons to avoid choosing, to avoid change, but we do not want to live a life full of fear.

Indecision or avoidance can stem from a fear of change itself. Pushing past our comfort zone triggers fear of the unknown, and change always involves an element of risk. We fear change when we view it as an exchange, attempting to predict whether we will be trading up and improving the situation, or whether we will regret the choice, judging it as a step in the wrong direction. But the beauty of change is that it will always provide an opportunity for something new, for growth, and the ability to learn. Once we become comfortable with making decisions, we learn to navigate the period of transition, the effect of the change.

Each ending is a beginning, the two are intertwined. Gilda Radner described periods of endings and beginnings as a 'delicious ambiguity'. But the ambiguity becomes a burden when it stems from an inability to allow an ending, to step away from the past, dragging our heels along the journey. We struggle with anything new because we desperately hold onto the old, comparing what it was, terrified to know that it will not be the same. Tyler Knott Gregson wrote, 'Oh what we could be if we stopped carrying the remains of who we were'. If we could release the dregs, the shadows of the past, we could allow ourselves to heal, within ourselves, and the world around us.

The resolution and evolution is what makes life so beautiful. There is true beauty in the transition of growth. Heraclitus said, 'No man ever steps in the same river twice, for it's not the same river and he's not the same man.' Phrased another way, Thomas Wolfe said, 'You can't go home again.' We strive to recreate relationships, feelings, memories, and circumstances, and we feel disappointed when they fail to match the original event. But you cannot go home again, because you are not the same person. We grow, change perspective and outlook. We cannot recreate old magic; we must create room for new, and trust that what we create can be even more beautiful than we can know.

I have friends who deny themselves opportunities to celebrate or indulge, because it would make the experience of fun 'less special', believing that the magic will run out and that life will become dull. As if life could ever be boring! We fight change because of fear, but we are designed for evolution. Even your DNA knows how to evolve. So if you are opting for the sidelines, you are just resisting the inevitable, and all of the rewards that accompany your evolution.

In reality, we are probably never fully ready to experience change, to evolve or grow, but we can embrace the opportunities that change provides. However, we must first begin to release our ideas about identity, of who we are supposed to be, and the way that life is meant to unfold. I do not think that we really change as individuals. But I know that as we allow ourselves to evolve, we release enough labels, fear, and limitation to become more fully who we truly are. What if we could see life changes as a way to bring us back to ourselves? What if we could change gears and receive the blessings that life has to offer?

On some level, most of us believe that in order to create, we have to destroy, and we are terrified of the chaos that would ensue. But destruction is an illusion, and we must remember that nothing is truly destroyed. Physics shows us that energy simply changes; we know that emotions evolve with relationships, and that we all simply evolve—nothing truly disappears from existence. We are afraid that change will either limit us, or that the chaos caused will overwhelm. So how can you navigate change without overwhelm? By choosing to flow with it, instead of fighting the current.

When we live in fear, we become stuck in a perpetual circle. The cycle never really changes because false is false. We may experience different manifestations of false, but if we are living on the surface, and there is no depth to our interactions because they are based on a lie. The reality is that we are here to evolve—it is in our DNA, the collective consciousness, and we constantly strive for it on some level. If we are fighting against our freedom, our ability to choose, then we are fighting existence itself.

Chapter 8: The Influence of Obligation

Life is a stage and we are the players. Shakespeare knew this, as have the greatest philosophers and teachers from every age. As we establish identity, we find the nuance of how it shifts with each person or environment we encounter. This makes sense, as our behaviour differs when interacting with our mother than that of a stranger, our best friend from school, or the work colleague we struggle to connect with. We are often drawn to or repelled by people because of what they 'bring out in us'. We might feel most excited about those who bring out our adventurous side, surround ourselves with those who help us to feel secure and accepted, and we might avoid those we consider to be negative because we believe they alter our mood. We can feel like twenty different people by the end of the day, due to how we interact and respond to others.

One of the biggest complaints I hear from my clients about other people is that they are parasites, they drain focus and energy, they are needy, or that they are manipulative or deceitful. We can often feel sucked into another's story and respond in ways that compromise our own sense of wellbeing. There are times when we attempt to respond with love and compassion, but often we match the lower energy that is presented.

When a friend tells you that she was yelled at by her boss at work, what is your normal response? Do you feel all-encompassing compassion for everyone involved, or is your immediate reaction to agree that she is a victim, has been horribly treated, and should feel very sorry for herself? We want to support our loved ones, to help them feel better, and try to appeal to them by matching the emotion or energy that they are in. And they often expect us to! We share stories because we want a reaction, to feel unburdened, a clearer understanding of how we feel, or we may want another to reinforce our sense of right and wrong. What about those around us who are acquaintances, or someone we feel less connected with? Are we more likely to dive into pity with them, or to oppose this, and instead try to push them away? We react according to the person and the situation, but again, often in ways that match the present vibration.

I often work with very sensitive people who believe that they are constantly under attack. They are always on the lookout for manipulation, from fear of being taken advantage of. Living 'on guard' is exhausting, and if we spend our lives trying to fight off others, we create barriers to having any kind of relationship, and excluding the ones we really desire.

With each of these situations, we can feel obligated to respond in a set way, to follow the script. We can play the role of the 'supportive friend', the 'flexible boss', or the 'dutiful son'. We listen to the pain and suffering and respond with pity, concern, or we try to fix it. We can also get so fed up with listening, or the demands to fix, that we can overcorrect and reject the person. It can be so easy to get caught up in the drama, and feel that we are then made to be the victim, that we are made to play the part that the other wants.

But remember, we are all just trying to feel better. We choose behaviours that we believe will lessen the pain, ease the suffering, make us feel stronger, smarter, better. We often do it in ways that are more damaging, such as excessive drinking or eating, or dumping our issues onto others, but we do this because we want to feel better. So when we feel that another person is trying to 'suck us dry', it is worth remembering that hurt people hurt people, that a lot of what we are perceiving is not being done to make us feel worse, but because they need help, love, and attention.

The key is to look to the bigger picture and understand what needs are not being met, for the other person, but also for us. Think back through your closest relationships, particularly to times when you felt insecure, or doubted your worth. What did you try to demand of your partner? Which ways did you push, stir, provoke, in order to make them prove his or her love to you? You may be pushing the boundaries of another, because you want to know that a person will love you, even when you are at your worst. We test because we do not trust that the connection will hold.

I know you have watched movies where a person has to walk across a frozen pond, or a very old suspended bridge. What do the characters do? They inch out to check that it will hold. They begin to apply more pressure, to bounce a little, and take heavy steps over the surface. We are constantly looking for the breaking point, and when we do not fully understand our boundaries, or the boundaries of another, we will push until that person pushes back, or the connection breaks.

Or we can go another way, and become overly generous. Have you ever bought someone a drink so that they would spend time with you? Have you bought someone a coffee so that you would have permission to 'pick their brain'? Or do something as a favour, and then become angry when the favour was not repaid? Unconsciously, we create deficits with others, and then wait to make sure they balance the scales. It is generous to share, to support, to give gifts to your friends, but when it creates a sense of debt or imbalance, this can cause more stress than appreciation.

We are all trying to feel better, to have our needs met, and we play the roles that have been written for us. Or not. The alternative, of course, is to choose to respond in a loving way, without bowing to the obligation or expectation. We have free will to choose our response. How often are we consciously choosing our responses, instead of reacting in the way that we 'should'? I am always amused by friends, sharing what they *should* say or do, while rolling their eyes, or trying to shrug it off. What does 'should' even mean? It indicates that there is an option, but pressure, either external or internal, to follow suit. How often does following the external 'should' make us feel better? It may relieve guilt or burden for a period of time, but it does not end there. As long as we bow to obligation or expectation, the pressure continues. Obligation is a heavy burden to carry, dictating a need to obey, to avoid conflict or confrontation.

What if you could see beyond the script and write your own lines, be your own character? What would change for you? What would change within your relationships? What if you knew that this was actually the most compassionate way to live your life for yourself, and those you love?

One of the hardest things to do is respond to a loved one in a way that could be perceived as rejection. When we stop agreeing that our friend is a victim, or when we stop feeling sorry for them, we can feel vulnerable. But agreeing with their fears is not compassionate, it just feeds fear, and they will keep behaving in the same way, because they feel that they are receiving the attention or love they desire. If we actually met their fear with love, they could learn that we love them, even if they stop playing the role of victim, bully, aggressor, or child. We can respond to the pain with a real dialogue, addressing ways to create change, or reconsider ways of thinking. Or we can simply tell them that we hope it gets better, and that we are here to provide love and support, no matter what. And instead of relying on a friend to participate with mean gossip, or needing them to tell us that we are right, smart, talented, we can choose to have a real conversation around the ways we may have contributed to a problem, and the action we can take to resolve it.

Obligating others to respond in unhealthy ways is another way to shirk responsibility, and ultimately delay our own growth. When we try to fix another person, we delay an opportunity for them to learn, to be empowered to choose a different experience. Choosing not to react to the prescribed roles is the most expansive expression of sharing the stage.

Entanglement

One of the most difficult areas of discernment revolves around entanglement and our interplay with others. Our empathy helps to provide clarity and a grounded, practical understanding of what another person is experiencing. For the very sensitive, problems arise when the lines become blurred between what is 'me', and what is 'you'. Have you ever walked down the street and inexplicably felt angry, or a sinking sadness? Or possibly energised and lifted? Or can you simply remember having conversations which you started, in a very good mood, but after sharing a space with another, you felt drained or deflated? Our empathy may be one of our greatest gifts, but when we are unclear about the source of the emotion, we can feel very confused.

Another common problem goes beyond the influence of interactions upon how we feel, to how we think and respond. How often do you find yourself agreeing with another, but after reflection, realise that you do not? While in the moment of the interaction, you found yourself nodding your head, agreeing with the statements, but not actually aligned with the line of thought? We each have extraordinary ability to influence the energy, the people, and the world around us. And we can also allow ourselves to be influenced if we are not aware of what truly aligns and what does not.

I remember joining an event filled with people who were quite stagnant and very complacent about manifesting change. Members of the group would talk about how their lives had not grown or evolved in five years, but they were determined that if they just keep doing what they had been doing, things would change. It was a memorable day for me because I had not been surrounded by this level of unwillingness in a long time. It was also memorable because within that group, I had a difficult time responding in the ways I would normally respond. I found myself starting to agree with, or say things that I did not really mean. I actually had to take a few minutes away to figure out what was going on inside of my head. I realised that I was reacting to the ways they were feeling, and to their thought patterns, and not my own.

There is a huge difference between *reacting* to someone, and *responding* to them. When we react to a person, we are speaking or acting because of what has been said or done. Our reaction is based off another's intention, feeling, choice, or action. Reacting to others will exhaust us, because we are always trying to balance the relationship, or keep some form of peace. But *responding* to another allows us to be fully aware of our thoughts and feelings, and clear of our intention as we interact. When we react to a person's pain, we do not take the pain from them. We feed the pain. When we react to a person's anger, we prove that anger provides a result. What if we could respond to the essence of that person instead? What if we could see the bigger picture and respond in the way that feels honest and aligned? As we respond to the being, instead of the projection, we honour them, and simply remind them of who they truly are. As we choose to respond, we choose our own experience, and share with the world. Choose not to react to their paradigm, and choose to live your own.

Part II:

Choose Your Boundaries

Chapter 9: Resistance

We set our boundaries as we make our choices. Setting a boundary is choosing an experience. The choices we make can impact daily life in a small way, or revolutionise it all. The bigger the choice, the bigger the impact, the more resistant we become to choosing, but I find that the real power comes in the smaller choices we make every single day. The culmination of the changes made in habit and attitude grow exponentially. The result is certainly greater than the sum of each small choice.

We diminish or delay change because of resistance. Think back to the last time you tried to make a big change, or multiple changes at once. Remember when you started a crash diet or detox, you joined a gym and threw yourself into it, or set a goal to write 2000 words per day? If you were already a healthy eater, a regular exerciser, or someone who wrote every day, the changes would not feel like such a stretch, and very possible with an added bit of effort. But when the change is too big, too fast, or you try to change it all at once, resistance rears its ugly head.

What is resistance really? We talk a lot about self-sabotage and avoidance and try to create strategies to fight it. But why do we experience resistance at all? We resist delving deep within, the pressure of deep diving. Have you ever seen what free divers do? Free divers go into the water, without oxygen, with only a few pieces of equipment, very little support. They can risk their lives to push the limits of their bodies, pushing themselves a little more each dive, to go deeper, longer, just to see what they can do, continually pushing the line between life and death.

Most of us are deeply afraid of anything that resembles this, but we emulate this behaviour as we push our comfort zones, and as we delve within ourselves. We are deeply complex, we are the sun and stars, blood and guts, fury and ecstasy, and this terrifies us. The duality becomes a whirlpool that we fear being sucked into, because we believe that we could never escape. But if we actually allow ourselves to go in, we learn to breathe in the depths.

Anaïs Nin wrote, 'I must be a mermaid, Rango. I have no fear of depths and a great fear of shallow living.' I believe that we each choose to become mermaids, or suffer living in the shallows. Making an expansive choice, will never result in shallow living. As we spend more time in the depths, we lose our taste for the shallows. Each of us are the ebb and flow of water, moving in and out from shore. As we release the need to be tethered to the shore, we discover the beauty of depth, and of ourselves.

The space between the two is the difficult part to navigate. The uncertainty and hesitation in choosing what is known and what is possible is what we all face, sometimes daily, but certainly continuously through life. We fear drowning, without recognising that we have been pushing our limits, understanding our strengths, and the desire to stretch ourselves beyond our known.

Choose to Act

In order to make a choice, we must understand our motivations, which requires us to be very honest with ourselves. Honesty is a courageous step, as we then recognise all of the ways that we have failed before. When I started to look at what I truly desired, the job I really wanted to have, the life I really wanted to live, I began to question everything about my life. We are afraid to question ourselves, because we then feel very vulnerable. We fear that everything could change, and too much change at once is terrifying. We fear that if we have not been honest in one area of our lives, we will find the same in other areas. And that is likely true to some degree, but we then have an opportunity to align what does not.

Looking at the bigger pictures helps us to identify the areas that are meaningful. This usually includes home, work, physical health, family, romantic partnerships, friendships, leisure time, money, and potentially a few others, depending upon individual circumstances and experience. In most cases, identifying one area out of alignment will also help highlight other areas that are as well. In order to gain harmony overall, the alignment of multiple areas will need to be addressed, because everything connects. Nothing in life is wholly independent of the rest of it. This is why an issue with money, a boss, trouble finding a home, and chronic headaches can all actually rooted in the same issue. As one area improves, another does as well. In many ways, this simplifies issues that we believe are very complex, and helping us recognise that deep down, there is always a simpler answer. The answer lies in looking at our choices.

As we become more aware of the *why* behind choices, we gain clarity in motivation, and also what has been healing over the years. Usually, we either try to fix everything at once, overwhelming ourselves in the process, or we just try to sort out one thing, but only on the surface, and only the symptom. By delving deeper, we can begin to understand the motivation causing the problem and address the true cause, instead of simply reacting to the symptoms created.

As a practitioner, I have worked with thousands of people wanting help with resolving their barriers. A small percentage returned with the same barriers, refusing to allow change. I worked with a woman who wanted to sell her business. Over the course of a few sessions, we resolved the emotional ties, the worries around letting it go, confusion over how best to prepare herself, and every other aspect she could come up with. We ran out of problems to address. At that point, she was simply at the stage where she needed to take action.

One of the biggest reasons for needing resolution or healing comes from an inability to act in authentic alignment. I know people who heal the same issues over and over again, having addressed family patterns, trauma from childhood, cultural influence. They finally stopped needing to heal these issues once the decision was made to also change their *behaviour*. When we choose differently, and act differently, we stop having to heal ourselves. We keep having to heal the same issues because we continue to choose to behave in ways that are not aligned.

How passive are you in speaking, acting, or making decisions? This could be your biggest area for growth. We can be overly passive, avoiding choice, which is, of course, a choice in itself. It is a choice to disengage with life. What I have consistently found is that the most 'laid back' of people are not. Deep down, they tend to be very anxious, because they are compensating, trying to relieve the anxiety by opting out. I used to be very indecisive, but convinced myself that I was easy to get along with. When I was honest with myself, I saw that I was letting my friends make choices because I did not want to be difficult, picky, or risk having my opinion ignored. I allowed opportunities to pass by, because I felt unable to choose, and decided not to. As we begin to lean into choosing, we begin to set boundaries in areas that we never have before. We choose how we want to feel, the ways we want to respond, and ultimately the way that we live and thrive.

Chapter 10: Establish & Maintain Boundaries

Establishing a boundary, making a choice and applying it, is an act of courage, requiring us to live consciously, with purpose. The more we understand ourselves and what aligns, it becomes possible to make conscious and subconscious choices, creating a life *on purpose*. How much of your life has been a 'mistake', or simply an acceptance of whatever was on offer? To establish a boundary, determine the desired outcome, what will be expansive in experience, and choose what will allow the experience.

After establishing a boundary, the next step is maintaining the choice, and there is a difference between simply establishing a boundary and maintaining it. Once a choice is made, there has to be an applied behaviour; it has to be followed through, to continue to live with the boundary. The beauty is that the decision only has to be made once, so all that is required thereafter is the follow-through, simplifying a process that could feel difficult to maintain. Consistency with the choices allows the world around to align with them, and with you.

We employ the concept of cause and effect in our daily lives, and everything has a consequence. When choices are erratic or inconsistent, a result of confusion or fear, life becomes that way too. Life will respond to what we choose to create. Consider relationship dynamics that have felt confusing, created from mixed messages, resulting in different moods for different days, and how it all began to stagnate. When our choices conflict, when we feel confused, the world around us can respond in the same way. The key is to identify our desires, and then make choices that will pave the way. Establishing a boundary is a powerful first step, but maintaining enables us to experience the benefits of the choices we make.

One of the most difficult aspects of maintaining a relationship is learning to navigate changes in boundaries, based upon change in circumstance. Our boundaries with a friend are straight forward, until she is promoted, or a professional relationship becomes personal as we deeply connect with a colleague, or a friendship evolves into romance. The period of transition, as with all aspects of life, can feel awkward or unnatural as we leave the comfort of a simpler dynamic, and deepen the connection.

A lot of us see ourselves as 'wearing hats'. We wear a work hat, a friend hat, a mentor hat, a parent hat, and behave in the way the role dictates. But if you are married to your business partner, who was also your best friend, and you are also a new parent, how do you choose which hat(s) to wear? The stack grows and we then spend energy and focus trying to balance the roles. Needless to say, the hat metaphor can only work with the surface of relationship dynamics. We actually have to understand where the roles meet, overlap, and create harmony between them.

Harmony or Balance?

How often do you ask for more balance in your life? I spent years trying to find balance and it was exhausting. I began to delve into the energy of balance, and then I understood why true balance felt impossible. Because it is.

Consider the facets of your life: work, partnership, friendships, physical health and wellbeing, leisure activities, sleep, travel, holidays, money, sex, education. When we start to consider them all, the circus comes to town. We have to master juggling, plate spinning, while walking the tightrope and racing to beat a timer. Balance means adjusting to all of the factors in our lives, giving them equal weight and influence. I gave up on balance because I realised I was chasing the impossible, and something I did not actually want. What I wanted, and what most of us really desire, is *harmony*.

With harmony, we can include as many facets as we choose, and each can occupy a different level of importance or impact. The focus with harmony is on releasing conflict and allowing ourselves to be a complex being, but without feeling overwhelmed. Balance is a compromise, and requires sacrifice, having *less than*. How much do you compromise in order to make life feel *in balance*? Striving for balance often fosters a feeling of defeat and disempowerment. When we choose harmony over balance, we benefit from the sum of all of our parts, instead of the few that we can cope with in the moment.

Chapter 11: External Validation

Before we courageously dive into openness and vulnerability, we often go through a period of testing the waters. The testing often creates a degree of drama, but we risk the discomfort to prevent a more severe pain. Our biology is wired to be cautious and so we choose baby steps over a leap of faith. We continue with this way of working through life in an attempt to remain connected with what we already know, as we inch toward what we are potentially ready to receive. We begin to gauge the effects of our new vulnerability by witnessing how others respond.

Viewing the world around us as a mirror can often be a useful tool. This may not work in every situation or with every person, because each of us is the centre of our own story, but we can certainly learn about ourselves through our interactions with others. In playing out the dynamics between ourselves and another, we can begin to gauge what is comfortable, what is accepted by others, and what is acceptable to ourselves.

For example, have you ever bought a new outfit, gotten a new haircut, or changed your interaction with another, just to witness the response? And did you go back to your original style when it was not well received? Or did a positive response give you the courage to continue with the new expression? We test the waters by witnessing another's response, depending on who we believe is important in our own lives. We may not care about the response of a stranger on the street, but our partner's disapproval can shake us to the core. What if our interactions with others serve to test the limit of a boundary, or just how vulnerable we can be without being stopped by fear?

We can identify the friends who push us to the limit of patience or compassion. We can recognise the habits of others that irritate or infuriate us, and boss who, yet again, has taken us for granted. We also act in ways that we know, deep down, push other people's buttons. We may do things to annoy our best friends, such as turning up late to meet them. We may ask them to do things for us that are over and above what could be expected. We can even demand that our friends drop everything in order to lift our spirits or make us feel better. When we push our loved ones, it is often just to test whether there is a limit to their love.

We talk a lot about unconditional love within the 'spiritual' sphere. We strive for perfect love, blind love, love without barrier, and we fail every day. As human beings, I question whether this is ever totally possible. Not because I doubt the human capacity for love, because I have witnessed infinite love and see it in others every day. But as long as we respond to our beliefs about who to love and how, we will continue to fall short of unconditional. We love our mothers in a different way to our teachers, friends, partners, or leaders. We believe that it is acceptable to withhold love from a criminal or an addict, but not from a sibling. Our beliefs about love and connection are the very barriers that we are fighting against.

Love is simply compassionate, healing, and light, but we attach so many expectations, obligations, and strings, that we are unable to experience love in the way that we crave. Our higher selves have a clearer understanding of love without condition, and how to share freely. On our very best days we know we are capable of transcending our barriers and loving in a way that is all-encompassing. As human beings, we often fall short of the mark. But I do believe that we are wholly capable of touching that perfection.

When I think about striving for our best, I think of Michelangelo's *Creation of Adam*, with the outstretched arms of Adam and God. We always aspire to a higher understanding, and we do this, not by forgetting our humanity, but by finding the energy of love and creation within ourselves. Adam's lack of effort or understanding represents our human barriers. The earnest reaching of God shows us what is readily available, when we consciously decide to connect and to love.

Chapter 12: How to say no

As we begin to choose our experiences, our beliefs, our feelings and perception, we are faced with the simple option of *yes* or *no*. The details may be complex, but ultimately we choose the option that will best serve. There seems to be a clear progression in how we begin to choose and establish a boundary, and it usually begins with first identifying the *no*.

Most of us begin to consciously choose our experience by first deciding what we do *not* want. We begin to set healthy boundaries by saying *no*, which often offers immediate relief, and can be the easier fix, when the relief is greater than the fear of saying no.

When choosing to opt out, or refuse an option, most of us fall into one of two categories. Some of us readily say *no* to almost everything, which is simply a protective reflex that stops us from having to consider a decision, or potentially regret a change. Automatically or overly rejecting the opportunities presented produces a small and unchallenged life. We can experience relief on one level, but also a lack of fun, connection, and the excitement, that new challenges can bring.

The second group struggles to say *no,* they are the 'rule followers', the conformists, and usually do anything and everything that is asked. The members of this group may be seen as the dependable, the 'fixers' who save the day, and who take great pride in these identities. But there will also be fear underlying an inability to say no when there is a better choice. Often, saying no can feel like the riskier option.

When you struggle to set a boundary by choosing to refuse a request, are you able to identify what is stopping you? What are your biggest fears around saying no? What would happen if you did? Do you know what a *no* feels like, or have you ignored or avoided this option throughout your life?

When I ask clients these questions, I am given a variety of answers, but they all ultimately boil down to fear, most often a fear of rejection. Most of us, on some level, will do what we can to make others happy, without truly understanding the cost to ourselves or our own wellbeing. We can feel that if we are not the ones fixing, sorting, doing for others, we will lose our place within the family, workplace, or relationship. When identity becomes entangled with what is done for others, it becomes harder to release the need to continue the behaviour. What if you could be accepted and appreciated for who you are, without having to sacrifice your happiness for another?

Another major issue revolves around our perceived obligations to another. We can often feel as though we have to continue with a pattern simply because that is the way it has always been. We 'loan' money to family members that we know will not be repaid. We cook and clean and work for another, knowing deep down that we will not receive what we want in return. We often do for others because we hope that it will evoke a response, or fulfil a need. We seek appreciation or recognition elsewhere because we do not receive it at work. We sacrifice in order to receive the love we did not have as children. But are these the best ways to receive what we are really seeking?

The feelings experienced around saying *no* are often some of the most uncomfortable. Many feel guilt or shame if they tell another that they are unable or unwilling to continue with a pattern that no longer serves. Often we can feel selfish for thinking of ourselves. But the benefits outweigh the perceived risk. The biggest benefit of saying *no* is that it creates a spaciousness within. Think of it as decluttering the energetic or emotional self. When we let go of an item of clothing, we create space for something new. Decluttering our home, evaluating possessions—whether they are still loved or enhance life—allows us to release the past and create space for the future. The pair of jeans that have been held onto for 10 years, which reflected an identity a decade ago, is no longer something that is needed. We can love specific times in our lives and the memories they evoke, but without relying on them to keep the past alive. Ultimately, this is a choice to be present, instead of living in the past.

Our physical world, especially our homes, or where we spend the majority of our time, show a direct reflection of our internal selves. If we feel confused, cluttered, or overwhelmed, our spaces can look and feel the same. As we make choices to release the clutter from one, we do the same in the other. Our internal space feels relieved, lighter, freer when we declutter our homes. We feel the same when we meditate, or resolve an ongoing struggle.

Just as we can outgrow possessions, we can outgrow connections, relationships, communities, and careers. Or it may simply be a case of allowing them to evolve and change into something new. As we evolve, boundaries also evolve and change, and as we establish boundaries with others, they are provided an opportunity to learn and evolve as well. Those we identify as boundary pushers, or as parasitical, are largely unaware of how their behaviour is impacting upon others. Remember, people are choosing words and actions they believe will make them feel better. So it does not mean that they are purposefully trying to hurt others, but they simply may not know of another way to receive attention. What if choosing healthy boundaries could show others how to connect in loving and respectful ways? Could this take some of the guilt out of the process?

As you reflect on your relationships with those around you, how do you generally feel that you are treated? Do you feel under-appreciated, disrespected, unheard? What are the common behaviours of others that are the most triggering? As you begin to identify what causes you to feel 'less than', you start to see where you can change a boundary. Disrespect, being dismissed, being interrupted, feeling excluded, dishonoured, undervalued, burdened, cluttered, or distracted are all aspects of life that you can live without. What aspects, choices, or behaviours are you ready to let go of?

What do you permit in the name of Patience?

I think that most of us mistakenly allow others to take advantage of us under the guise of patience. Over the years I have repeatedly asked for patience, wanting to feel calm and compassionate in the face of various levels of abuse. I asked for patience with clients who were deceiving themselves about their state of health and wellbeing, for when I was delayed because of another, and when a friend began to push and then shove against my boundaries.

I believed that I needed to be more patient in these situations, but patience was not the answer. The answer was *courage*. I needed courage to choose a reaction that would influence the dynamics that had become increasingly unhealthy. I have listened to teachers preach the power of patience: 'Be patient, what you have been asking for will come to you'. I believe that this works to the degree in which we can allow, and then it is up to us to meet the universe halfway, to do our share. Patience must be paired with courage, as taking an overly passive approach to life will have you sitting on the sidelines, watching it all go by.

True patience allows us to interact with a degree of detachment. This allows us to connect without being overwhelmed by judgement. Patience provides us with the capacity to receive another person, with all of her flaws, without dismissing her because of them. It means letting go of judgement in favour of an opportunity for a second chance, for another interaction that is enjoyable, or more aligned. Patience will continue to provide opportunity for a relationship to evolve, and in that sense, patience is priceless. Consider your friends, especially the ones that you possibly did not like upon first meeting. One of my best friends from university thought that I was sarcastic and rude when she first met me. Luckily, she was patient enough to try again, and two decades of friendship have followed. Patience keeps our judgments from setting and hardening, like cement. A degree of patience in our lives will always serve us, but the challenge is to ensure that we are engaging patience without being passive.

Sacrifice, Burden, & Responsibility

We all strive to be the best version of ourselves, to serve the world, to inspire the best. When we do so from the highest intention, we live as our higher selves. But what if we are choosing to act from fear, or a misunderstanding of the virtues we are attempting to apply?

History, religious texts, and even children's books are full of stories of sacrifice, where the hero places another's life above his own. But sacrifice and suffering, committed in the name of love, is blasphemy. We hear stories of lovers, parents, pets sacrificing on extraordinary levels for the ones they love. The idea is romantic, and we fall in love with the story. We want to believe that there is a possibility that someone would love us enough to do the same. But when we romanticise, we actually dishonour the love within the act. We love the story instead of understanding the motivation that created it.

Sacrifice is a concept that is often touted as the answer to ills, the missing piece. Parents sacrifice to give their children what they never had themselves, partners sacrifice aspects of their own happiness or fulfilment, and culturally, and as a species, we emphasise the importance of sacrifice. Human beings have a tendency to get caught in the cycle of give and take, relying upon cause and effect, like for like, and exchange in order to gain. As a result, we also believe that we must sacrifice happiness now in order to experience it in the future. We work extra hours, sacrificing time and energy, sacrificing freedom, believing that to receive, we must first give. We sacrifice spontaneity in order to save a bit of money or time. We make choices based on sacrificing now, so that another can have, and as a result, we stop ourselves from living a fuller existence. The reason that we sacrifice for others is because we feel responsible for them. We endeavour to make another happy, fulfilled, whole, and we sacrifice our own happiness and fulfilment in the hope that this will happen, because we hope that it will also make us feel better.

Each of us is responsible for one person only: ourselves. Being responsible for others makes us feel important, wanted, or included, and giving up the need to be responsible for everyone is a scary prospect. But consider the difference between control and influence. We are absolutely able to influence another's experience, to contribute to a sense of happiness or wellbeing, but we cannot *make* another feel. We are unable to control another's thoughts, behaviour, emotional state, or choices. We do not have the power to control another's life. Our friends and family have free will and the ability to choose, which makes each of us responsible for ourselves. The choice of feelings, thoughts, and responses is each person's own responsibility.

When choosing to be responsible for ourselves solely, we are relieved of the burden of fixing it all. We free ourselves enough to choose ourselves, and this is the greatest gift we can give, to ourselves and the world. How much of the burden that you carry belongs to others? How much time do you spend worrying about your family? How much energy do you spend doing for others, without it having the impact you desired?

When we allow others to take responsibility for themselves, we bless them with the ability to learn, evolve, grow. The arrested development of our loved ones exists as a result of a refusal to take responsibility for oneself. And there is usually another person trying to be responsible for the individual, feeling more and more frustrated and desperate over time. We only arrest ourselves, and while we can receive support and guidance from others, ultimately, we can only change from within.

Most of us become arrested when we move into a passive stance, allowing others to do for us what we choose not to face. We can fall into the habit of waiting for others, almost needing permission to make a choice. The damsel in distress waits for her knight in shining armour to ride in, defeat the monsters, and carry her off to the castle, to live happily ever after. Are you waiting for the same?

On the other side, we can blame others for our own perceived shortcomings. We blame other people or circumstances, because we feel rejected, limited, or unhappy. We blame our partners because we feel unfulfilled in our relationships. We blame our bosses because we feel limited in our roles at work. We blame others, society, the world, because we fail to recognise that we have the power to change our own perception. This ability is the most empowering concept that we can ever understand or apply. What a relief to know that we do not have to change the entire world; we only need to change ourselves from within!

A few years ago, I attended a course with a man who pushed just about every trigger within me. I suffered through the first day, because I thought that he was rude, condescending, dismissive, and would not listen. I was impatient to leave class at the end of the day, so that I could spend time looking at why these behaviours triggered so much within me. Instead of blaming him for making me feel angry, frustrated, or upset, I looked within myself to understand. Introspection allowed me to let go of the need to either avoid him, or try to change him. The reality is that he has friends and family who love and accept him exactly as he is. It was my beliefs that were stopping me from doing the same. I resolved the conflict within myself, which allowed me to see him from a higher perspective, and appreciate him for the individual that he is, without the need to try to change him. I felt free, and the change in my perspective completely altered and improved our interactions.

By taking blame out of our lives, we release ourselves from the obligation of fixing others, or the entire world. As we recognise all the ways we sacrifice, the disharmony in responsibility, the burdens we carry, we can release ourselves from the constraints we feel. These are the heaviest, the most limiting dynamics within our lives, the ones that weigh us down. And as we release the burdens, we create a spaciousness that allows more choice. We free ourselves from limitation, from resentment, jealousy, blame and shame, from the feelings that cause the most discomfort, those least aligned with our higher selves. As we step out of burden and sacrifice, we create space for what we *do* desire. It is only when we create enough space to rise, to breathe, that we truly begin to live.

Chapter 13: Choose Your Yes

Mastering the art of saying *no* creates a feeling of spaciousness and clarity, which then allows us to say *yes*. Setting boundaries and releasing clutter allows us to find the necessary clarity, to identify what nourishes, body and soul. Letting go, releasing obligation, creates an opportunity to identify true desire. Saying no can be expansive, as you release specific aspects and allow yourself space to expand in other ways. The key to finding this clarity comes from within, learning to focus on the *feeling* more than the thought, to identify the desire, to consider how it will feel. This requires permission to imagine, and to consider a growing number of options. Just because relationships have been difficult in the past does not mean that has to continue. Just because work has been unfulfilling does not mean that it will remain so.

What do you *want*? What could you say an enthusiastic *yes* to? Consider the various aspects of your life, your relationships, your work, your lifestyle and how you spend your time. What would you love to amplify in each of these? Choosing your *yes* is about making yourself the priority, choosing *yourself*, and choosing what *feels* good to choose.

One of the biggest barriers to identifying or receiving what we desire is asking for something that we do not fully understand. We may be desperate for love, begging the universe for a soulmate, friends who love us, or a more compassionate existence. And we always get what we ask for. The problem comes from confusion or misunderstanding around what we request. It is possible on one level to understand the lightness and freedom that love embodies, but on another level associate love with abuse, pain, abandonment, or control. We see this repeatedly within our own relationships or those of others. We watch our friends continue to repeat the same relationship dynamics with different partners throughout their lives. They want true love, care, and respect, but end up in relationships that do not fulfil their desires. This is because of the discord between beliefs of what *love* really is.

We often ask, and receive a limited version of our request. We know friends who needed a break and were fired from their jobs, or who needed to rest and got sick, forcing them to rest. We know those who demand respect and unintentionally bully others, believing that respect comes from fear. The world is full of people who are asking for a positive experience, attempting to fulfil a need, but failing to find it because they do not truly understand what they are asking for.

Our first step is clarification of desire, and an opportunity to identify the source of our setbacks and confusion, so that we can have what our heart and soul desires. Saying *yes* is the most expansive way to live your life, once you are clear on what you accepting.

Respect & Honour

Growing up in the southeast of the United States, respect was a value that I was shown every day, based in appreciation and gratitude. When I look back at my childhood I am grateful for the foundations that it instilled in me, because I know they have shaped my life experience in uncountable ways. I know that each example is small, but they all taught me to consider how I treated others, and how I wanted to be treated in return. The Golden Rule tells us to do unto others as we would have them do unto us, and Confucius stated 'Never impose on others what you would not choose for yourself.' Following these simple instructions provides a great exercise in empathy and respect. The problems arise when we are not clear on what respect is, how to receive it, and how to share.

Respect, as with most virtuous aspects, begins with the ability to see the highest perspective of another person. We often fail to fully understand another, or understand the dynamics of the relationship, because our beliefs become a barrier to the higher truth. Respect stems from an admiration of another, which could be based on the favourable or valued qualities, but also the ability to see another from the highest perspective. Respect is then inspired, as a foundational piece of any healthy relationship, with a partner, friend, sibling, or community.

We respect others when we decide what we want to experience within a relationship. F. Scott Fitzgerald wrote, 'If you spend your life sparing people's feelings and feeding their vanity, you get so you can't distinguish what should be respected in them'. When we are honest with ourselves about the types of behaviours and people that inspire us, it becomes easy to choose. We disrespect ourselves and others when we hide our feelings, or continue to indulge a lack of respect.

When I worked for the Department of Juvenile Justice, I saw firsthand the lack of empathy and respect for others, the community, and more importantly, for the young people themselves. Within each child or parent I spoke to, there was a lack of understanding around how certain behaviours could impact others or the community itself. There was always a lack of respect because there was a lack of understanding, stemming from a lack within themselves. When we can begin to truly respect ourselves and then the world around us, our behaviour changes; but this all starts from within, from that higher knowing.

If we take respect a step deeper, we find the essence of *honour*. Honour includes a deep love and admiration, it is ancient, and this understanding within our ancestors is a source of some of these greatest gifts and deeply held values. One of my favourite aspects of working with others is hearing about their families, histories, and how they, as individuals, have been shaped by their ancestry. We know that we inherit patterns of thought and behaviour which may, or may not, be helpful in our contemporary lives. We carry old prejudice and fear from ancestors who fought in wars, whose lands were invaded, or who simply were unable to accept a tradition or custom outside of their own. However, some of our greatest treasures lie within our DNA. When we begin to recognise that we inherited our smile and sense of humour from our grandmother, our curiosity and need for truth from our grandfather, or learn that our great-great grandfather was an explorer, explaining our wanderlust, we begin to value our ancestry and ourselves on a deeper level.

I have facilitated courses and workshops, delving deeply into the DNA, uncovering and understanding family patterns and problems, and these are always among the most fascinating and beautiful experiences. We can feel the resolution of centuries of heartache and pain through the family line, and the gratitude that is felt within the family for the healing that is experienced. It is truly an honour to witness others heal the family line, not by blaming the ancestors for their shortcomings, but by understanding what their ancestors could not.

When we begin to accept others, and accept them for their flaws as well as their gifts, we begin to ease into honour. Respect is required to truly understand honour, and honour is the deepening of the acceptance and love inherent. When you consider honour, what comes to mind? What does it look like, feel like? How could it change your life? Take a moment to connect with your DNA, your ancestry. What can you recognise that is worthy of respect? And are you able to honour it all?

Love, Compassion, & Deep Connection

Do you truly understand *love*? On some level, we all fight it. We ask for, beg and plead for love, and then reject loving experiences as they are offered. There is always a complex mix of ideas, pictures, and feelings that float to the surface as we consider love. The layers of misaligned ideas are the result of millennia of human beings trying to grasp at love, but failing to understand it.

As we develop relationships with partners, lovers, friends, we all truly want one thing: love. But we fail in our attempts to inspire, create, cajole, or evoke love within ourselves or another, because we have too many conflicting beliefs about what love really is.

Those who have been in abusive relationships will associate love with abuse. If 'the people who love you, leave you', we believe that love leads to abandonment. We have associations based on our experiences, but we are blaming love for the areas in which love has actually been lacking. Love does not create abuse, pain, manipulation, fear, neglect, abandonment, or any other negative association we could create. Love is what heals them. As we begin to release these associations, we allow ourselves to experience all that love will offer freely.

Consider the loving relationships that ultimately ended. Take a moment to connect with just one period of time, or even just one moment, when the love felt untainted and pure. We all know love because we all have the capacity for love, it is in all of us, and is the best of us. Anytime we have a moment of transcendence, of seeing life beyond the little details, we are remembering *love*. We can always remember the love that was experienced, without confusing love with the pain from the relationship's ending.

When we begin understand and live with love, we engage compassion, and find freedom that we may never have known before. Acts of compassion, which can have a worldwide impact, or a simple small gesture, are what will ultimately change the world. I very recently stumbled upon a photography exhibition in Sorrento, with simple, candid, black and white pictures of Mother Teresa, spanning her life of service. The images were moving, an example of *living compassion*. She understood the energy of compassion in a way that most struggle to reach, and she became a channel for love. We all have the ability to reach that potential, once we decide to touch it, feel it, and then live it. The greatest of goals? Absolutely one worth reaching for, and living.

Imagine that all of your relationships were created in the energy of love and compassion. What would change? My guess would be, *everything*. We crave connection in a way that is primordial, and also divine. Our human selves demand attention, affection, and recognition in order to prove that there is connection, but a false sense of *meaningful* connection. Meaning does not stem from the evidence that we can see, but from what is felt within, what changes and heals us. Consider the ways that you try to evidence connection in your life: wedding rings, friendship bracelets, Facebook friend requests, invitations to parties, clothing featuring your favourite band, joining a class, learning the lingo of a particular sub-culture, are all ways that we try to prove connection and inclusion, and we feel devastated if we are not met with open arms.

There is a lot to say for setting the tone ourselves, instead of responding to others. I spent my middle and high school years trying different sports, classes, community groups, participating in choir and musicals, in an attempt to find the right fit. I had a lot of friends, but always felt a little on the outer edge, nothing was quite right. Connection begins within. When connected and integrated yourself, you begin to connect with others who love and appreciate you, on a new level. There is a difference in responding to what another can give you, and allowing yourself to set the tone for more loving connection.

The Power of Freedom

We often fall into the trap of 'playing' with power because we want to play the game. Every human being on this planet has the privilege of applying freewill to life, because each of us has free choice, and we choose our experiences. We choose who we interact with, we choose how we feel, what we believe, where we live, what we eat, and are the most powerful beings in our world. So this gives rise to the question: how is it possible to feel like a victim, or weak, discouraged, afraid to change?

In an attempt to learn, we gauge our experiences through comparison and contrast. We often judge our level of power based on how much influence we have over another. We believe that if we do not have the upper hand, we are being controlled. But having the upper hand, or the ability to 'control' another, is not real power. True power is based in love, respect, and honour. The reality is that we cannot control another, and another cannot control us. We can believe what we choose, and empower ourselves only when we stop believing what simply is not true. We feel controlled, limited in our choices, because we are avoiding feeling afraid. We see this in our own relationship dynamics, but also in how the world responds to attacks, war, and acts of violence. Our subconscious inclination is to avoid the pain and suffering, and to stay in our little corner, so that our own power, or feeling of strength is not disturbed.

Power is not fighting, or feeling that you have to defeat every bully that the world produces. Power comes from really knowing yourself and your values enough to know that they are unshakable, indestructible, and ultimately, in living within your alignment. We only feel threatened when we slip into fear. We only feel weak when we compromise ourselves. Abuse of power is not really power, it is using fear to influence, but we can only be influenced when we allow it. As we choose to respond in fear, we step out of power. When we choose from a place of understanding and strength, we change the dynamics of power within a relationship. Anything that challenges our sense of power provides an opportunity to learn more about it. When have you felt powerful or strong? What contributed to that feeling?

I know that the moments you felt the most powerful were also the moments you were most at peace. Peace is *powerful*. A lot of us associate peace with being walked over, giving up, or letting others have what they want by sacrificing ourselves. But the most peaceful people in the world are those who are totally aligned with what they think, say, and do. Peace comes as a result of a resolution of inner conflict, which comes with self-acceptance. What are you fighting against that is disturbing your peace? True alignment comes as a result of accepting our power and living in peace.

Chapter 14: The Risk and the Payoff

Stepping into power and peace also requires us to be vulnerable. When you think about allowing yourself to be vulnerable, what do you feel? Most of us have a deep fear of vulnerability. We associate vulnerability with weakness, being taken advantage of, having no choice, or feeling trapped. We associate pain and suffering from the past with periods of vulnerability. We judge childhood as a vulnerable time, when we were at the mercy of our parents or other adults, unable to choose for ourselves, and living a life full of others' ideas and barriers. But this is not true vulnerability.

Being vulnerable simply requires us to be *open*. It does not mean accepting all behaviour, all treatment, any form of abuse. It means allowing ourselves to be open to possibility. How many times have you asked for more love in your life, for more abundance, freedom, or affection? And how many times have you slammed the door shut when these were offered? Many people preach the virtues of the Law of Attraction, exclaiming that you only have to ask and you will receive. They are on the right track, but often the issue is not in the asking, it is in the *receiving*. We cannot receive what we desire without being open to allowing. We cannot have what we have been asking for, without choosing to experience it.

Many of us have become very detached from our hopes and dreams, and are able to identify what we want in only a very theoretical way. We imagine having loving relationships, a home that we appreciate and adore, the dream job, but it is too external to really connect with. As a result, we either struggle to manifest because we cannot feel the connection, or because we are unable to accept them when offered. Allowing ourselves to be vulnerable connects us with our deepest desires, because we are *in* them, totally immersed. Vulnerability embodies authentic connection and expression of ourselves, because we are then living and breathing our essence.

Surviving to Thriving

What is the key to truly living the life you love, to move from surviving to thriving? I think it begins with curiosity and fascination. How often do you discover that you feel bored, flipping through the channels, pacing, checking the refrigerator, or any other mindless, uninspired task? Boredom in itself is a kind of death. We are alive and breathing, but without much else to evidence life. In this beautiful, vast, complex, glorious world, there really is no excuse for boredom. There is too much to do, see, read, eat, try, experience in this world to feel bored. Boredom is the end of imagination, and stopping short of moving beyond your comfort zone.

The first step out of boredom is *curiosity*, when we begin to look beyond what is already known, and consider ideas and experience out of our current bubble of existence. When we find something that really clicks, we begin to experience a fascination, which can ignite passion. There has to be a newness, a sense of freshness for passion. We lose our passion for jobs and relationships because we fail to find a new facet within the familiar. Aspects of life become stale as we exhaust our ability to learn or grow, and fascination fades. Passion and fascination will only continue to be sparked as we search out new ways to live, learn, and evolve.

Once a passion is sparked, we are inspired to do, adding the necessary boldness to the mix. The first, and possibly most important, step towards becoming more bold, is applying *courage*. Courage requires us to face our fears, to become our own superheroes. In order to have any meaningful sense of healing or resolution, we must have courage, no way around, no bypass. The beauty is that, with courage, we are able to face our fears, recognise that they are lies, and move forward without the burden. Courage facilitates freedom on every level. And it helps us to step beyond our comfort zones, and into a bold existence. We are never totally without fear; we will face fear anytime we try something new. And because life is about diving into the shiny and new, there will always be a reminder that we are stretching ourselves. The key is to change our relationship with fear. Instead of considering something new, feeling fear, and giving up, it is possible to recognise that the fear is an acknowledgement, an application of courage, and move forward despite the fear. Be empowered by your courage, your ability to feel the fear, appreciate the indication, and move beyond.

Becoming comfortable with courage, and stretching beyond comfort allows us to increase spontaneity. When was the last time you did something that was truly spontaneous, without investing a lot of time into planning or preparation, when you followed your gut and heart, and just went for it? There is a little bit of magic in all that is spontaneous. Some of the best moments, or at least the best stories, start with a decision to dive in. The best nights out are unplanned. The best holidays are the ones that do not follow the itinerary.

When was the last time you felt thrilled over the possibilities? One of my best friends laughs at me, because anticipation is one of my favourite experiences. I love not knowing all of the details. Some of my favourite moments in life are those spent diving in and waiting to see what will happen. Going on first dates, applying for a big promotion, waiting to see how the world responds, is exciting and risky. Being spontaneous and enjoying the anticipation of witnessing the way life responds create an edge, but an edge that thrills instead of terrifies. This is the edge that gives way to adventure. The point of all of this is to embrace a life of adventure—why else would you be here? Allow yourself to thrive within the adventure of your life. Get as much out of it as you possibly can, be thrilled by the possibility of each day.

Abracadabra

The concept of *communication* often is underrated and misunderstood. Information is widely available on the importance of getting communication right, and resulting confusion and pain associated with a lack of clear communication. But the real importance of communication, or expression, is in its essence, and in its purpose.

Every relationship, every interaction, every choice is an expression. Tone, body language, style of dress, sofa type, model of car, books, movies, and music consumed all come as result of expression. As we consciously or unconsciously choose to express ourselves, we show the world what we want to experience. As we express ourselves, we call in our experiences.

Expression is an integral part of our creative experience, and engages our intention and creative energy at its core. Students often ask how best to manifest or receive what they desire. The first question I ask is 'What are you doing in your life right now that is creative?' The answer is usually very little, or sporadic acts. Our creative energy and our expression are linked, and unless we are using them both, they both suffer or stagnate.

We know that what we think and speak about are what we ultimately create. The word Abracadabra means 'I create as I speak', and we are always creating as we speak, and expressing our desires through our choices. As we choose, we create our experience. And as we create, we express new aspects of ourselves. It is a beautiful cycle, an ebb and flow, where we can grow exponentially through choosing to truthfully express ourselves, and can witness our lives unfold as other people, and the world, respond in kind. Move beyond the Law of Attraction, and delve into the depths of your true desires, embody them, become them, and create your world. The more we engage in creative acts, painting, singing, writing, building, sculpting, dancing, the more we show life that we are ready to apply the same intention and focus to ourselves. As we express ourselves through our creativity, we invite life to respond to our essence, the truest parts of ourselves.

Loyalty & Devotion

Loyalty is a beautiful virtue to embody and apply, but it only retains its beauty when we are loyal to that which aligns with our own values. How many times have you remained loyal to a friend or partner who consistently behaves in ways that you cannot condone? How often do you command yourself to suffer consequences because you feel that disagreeing with a friend would show that you are disloyal? We can be loyal to an idea, a way of life, a philosophy, and align ourselves with the actions and behaviour that are inspired by these ideas. We can also be loyal to a person who shares these. We do not have to be loyal to behaviours that conflict, even if they come from a person we feel loyalty towards. There is a fine line between loyalty and blindly following that which is not ethically or morally sound. Too many acts or words stem from what is claimed to be loyalty, but actually comes from a refusal to commit to one's own sense of integrity.

We can love a friend, be loyal to that deep connection, and disagree with a friend's actions. Loyalty does not require a refusal to see the truth of a situation. Many turn a blind eye to pain and suffering in the name of loyalty, and all they do is cheapen a deeply powerful virtue. Loyalty is never something to give blindly. The connection of loyalty must embody the best of who we are, and the best within another.

I have worked with clients who felt that they could not stand up to a partner, leave an abusive relationship, or be honest, because it would be a betrayal. They sacrificed their own right to choose, in the name of loyalty. I have seen friends take over the family business, which caused them heartache and sacrifice, because they felt that their version of loyalty was required to keep the family happy. I know that I have allowed friends to treat me in hurtful ways, and let it go, without a word, because it felt disloyal to criticise. Loyalty was never a part of any of these scenarios—but they were all opportunities to understand how to be loyal to others while also being loyal to oneself.

Loyalty is a powerful virtue, but I would choose *devotion* over loyalty every time. While loyalty can often feel like a duty, devotion feels divine. What if you were only willing to choose people, jobs, education, that you felt inspired enough to be devoted to? Devotion releases any need to *try* to be loyal, to debate our commitments, or to weigh up the options. It frees us of judgement or guilt. Devotion encompasses love and higher perspective and choice. Become devoted to your happiness, your health, your freedom, your priorities, and your life will never be the same.

Authenticity & Freedom

I believe that the word 'authentic' is one of our most sacred. It means genuine, original, and true. The biggest battles in our lives are the ones in which we fight to find and express what is true. The way is often filled with shadows and distraction, and we often are led down paths that look promising, but ultimately end in the disappointing realisation that we were trying to become someone other than who we *are*.

I am often asked about the healing process and why we must go through it. Our healing process, delving into the dark and understanding it, letting go of the past, is what allows us to find what is genuine. I believe that most of us correctly immerse ourselves in the process of healing, but then lose sight of the reason for it. When we allow ourselves to heal what is getting in the way of knowing, accepting, and embracing ourselves, we take our healing to a new level. That level is the key to our freedom. Fear is the lie, and finding the truth allows us to live an authentic existence. We only feel trapped when we are unable to share our genuine feelings or express ourselves in the truest sense. Freedom is the ability to *be,* *a*nd in our truest state, we are totally free.

We have become increasingly obsessed with self-improvement, and the idea that we must change. We are judged for staying the same, for refusing to push ourselves, or challenge the world around us. Instead, I would encourage you to focus on *evolution.* Our lives are a journey, and we are never really able to stay stagnant. I know quite a few people who are doing their best to stay in their own little bubbles, to avoid anything uncomfortable, but they fail on a daily basis. Not because they try to avoid, but because we simply cannot avoid. Evolution is inevitable; it is built into our DNA, and is part of why we are here. The truth is that we never really change. We simply move closer into alignment with who we really are. As we heal, we are more genuinely ourselves, and we are simply more integrated with truth. So our pressure to change is unnecessary. Simply choose evolution and move towards alignment with the original essence of *you.*

As we identify all that we can embrace in life, we begin to align more and choose more of what we want to feel and experience. As we understand what we want to feel, we begin to choose thoughts and actions that help to facilitate the feeling. Continuing to delve within, to discover and express ourselves, allows us to identify all that is necessary in our lives.

Chapter 15: Non-negotiable Priorities

Identifying and applying our 'non-negotiable priorities' is an expansive and grounded way to *live* the boundaries that we choose. The practical application of choice is what facilitates evolution for ourselves and daily life. Understanding what is a necessary part of our health, wellbeing, or happiness, and then knowing that we are worthy of scheduling the day around our priorities, will bring life into alignment with *us*.

How do you want to feel on a daily basis? You may have a long or varied list, as the different aspects may require or inspire a variety of feelings. You may want to feel focused at work, or calm and relaxed at home. You may want to feel as though you are learning and growing as you read and study, or that you are developing your mind or creativity as you practice playing the guitar. Consider your lifestyle, all that you do, but focus on how you want to feel every day.

Consider what is 'non-negotiable' in your life. Think about the events or experiences that brighten your day, enhance your life, and inspire happiness. These can be simple, such as going for a run, or attending an art class, or they can be much more grand, such as travelling the world, or stepping into a career that you truly love.

Think about all that helps you to feel healthy, harmonious, light, free. These could include exercise, healthy meals, juicing, meditation, rest, reading. You can even ask your body what it needs to have or do, in order to feel great. The first step is getting very clear on how you want to feel, and then finding inspired action that will contribute to the feeling.

Once we begin to establish the priorities in our lives in the way we want to feel, we can easily identify the actions that contribute. And once we identify the priorities and action, to make them a regular part of daily life.

The process of identifying non-negotiable priorities can be life changing, in every facet. Once we identify and apply them, we can stop arguing with ourselves about how we 'should' be spending our time. We often neglect our bodies because we think we should be working instead. We may neglect our sense of peace and ability to focus, because we believe that we have to answer every email as soon as it is received. Having clarity on what is really necessary to be happy and harmonious with all aspects of life allows us to give these a place, and arrange the other aspects around them. Focusing on your non-negotiable priories will help to make *you* the priority in your own life.

Here are a few prompts for and examples of setting non-negotiable priorities for yourself:

- How often do you need to exercise (per week) to feel fit or healthy? And would enjoyable exercise include a gym, a swim, a dance class, or a run?

- Is learning a priority? How do you love to learn? Are you happy to learn on your own, reading books, articles, completing courses online? Do you enjoy attending workshops with other like-minded individuals? Are you able to set aside time to read or learn on a regular basis, simply for the joy of it?

- What is the quality of your relationship with technology? Do you feel that your time and focus is dictated by your phone, laptop, or any other electronic device? Do you feel that you must be at the beck and call of the world? Would it be possible to set a limit on the number of times you check your email or other social media platforms each day?

Within each area of our lives, there are choices we can make, changes that will improve our relationship with ourselves and those around us. Consider each aspect of your life, and identify what is not working for you. What could you release, change, do differently, that would improve your state of being? And what positive experiences could you add or increase in frequency, to bring more joy, fun, or adventure into each day? Think about your daily, weekly, monthly, and yearly schedule as well. Consider your daily practices, like meditation, your commute, the job you do, the food you eat, and exercise you take. Also take the time to evaluate what you do on a less regular basis. Consider your social time, evenings out with friends, and aspects such as travel, holidays, and how you want to spend your free time.

You may need to juggle this around, and try a few different approaches. It is worth reconsidering your non-negotiable priorities every few months. Your body or spirit may not want to experience the same activities after some time. It may be right for you to take a dance class for a few months, and then try yoga or painting. But always make sure that you are setting a boundary so that you can explore these, giving yourself permission to take the time to play, create, and *do*, in your daily life. The point of a non-negotiable priority is not to get you stuck in a schedule that never changes. It is more about making yourself a priority in your own life, honouring what is best for *you*, and giving yourself permission to live and enjoy it! It is about having permission to play, to explore, create, express yourself, and create spaciousness that allows room for you in your own life.

Create a list of what you know you need to have or do in order to feel great. Consider daily, weekly, monthly, yearly priorities. And once you have identified them, write them into your diary. Give them space in your daily life.

Identify amazing relationships and connections. What makes them so great? What would feel amazing in a job or career? The ability to express yourself? Some independence? Meaningful influence? What makes your body feel ecstatic? What contributes to feeling relaxed? Strong? Useful and appreciated?

What is important for you to feel, experience, and embody?

Part III:

Live Your Calling

Chapter 16: Closing the Gap

The space between who we believe we are, and who we want to be, is what propels growth and evolution. It is the gap between our current state and our highest potential. It highlights the areas of misalignment, of disconnection, of being outside of the path of purpose. Navigating the space between is what will lead you back home.

Closing the gap is the greatest part of the journey back to ourselves—creating an extraordinary existence through experience, identifying what aligns, and consistently choosing all that does. As we identify each *yes*, we are more easily able to live what aligns. The process of finding and choosing is just like everything else worthwhile: it takes practice. Every day, we are provided opportunities to practice, to live, choose, and do. We are given a lifetime to learn.

Relationship with Time

Most of us have an awkward or uncomfortable relationship with time, which can cause frustration or drama on a daily basis. Time is a very fluid concept, an illusion, a perception. We know this because one moviegoer can feel that a film ends quickly, and to another, it drags on endlessly. We also know that in various circumstances, time seems to slow dramatically, so that we can take in more information and understand what is happening around us, as occurs in an accident when time seems to stand still. The problem is that so many of us see time as something that controls us, that we have to fight against, or desperately attempt to slow down. We race against the clock, run out of time, and we frequently worry about wasting our time. Time has an enormous influence on our daily lives, the quality of life, and our choices.

Albert Einstein said, 'The only reason for time is so that everything doesn't happen at once'. What if time actually allows us to experience events in an order that can be followed and measured, enabling us to perceive and interpret the events and their significance? What if time is one of the greatest gifts that this life has to offer? We are given time to process, time to learn, time to grow. Most of us work and live on a schedule, which can feel like an asset or a barrier, depending upon whether we have learned to make time work for us. Time is actually one of our biggest allies, one of the greatest gifts that we have, which we can appreciate once we change our relationship with it. When we feel as though we have to fight against it, rush against the clock, to hurry up, we are being motivated by fear. On some level, we are often trying to push ourselves to move into our calling.

Time is a beautiful, amazing gift that allows us a space to become more conscious, but works very differently beyond our little world. We are eternal and we are infinite. In this moment, you are everyone, everywhere, and everything. Did you know this? Can you feel it? Take a moment and allow yourself to feel all that you are in existence, beyond your human body.

We are often reminded to be present, and 'in the now'. We often struggle to reconcile the understanding of how to be here now, but also everywhere else, at every moment, at once. The two seem to contradict each other. Osho states that 'In the moment of love, past and future are no more. Then, one delicate point is to be understood. When there is no past and no future, can you call this moment the present? It is the present only between the two- between the past and the future. It is relative. If there is no past and no future, what does it mean to call it the present? It is meaningless. That is why Shiva doesn't use the word present. He says, everlasting life. He means eternity…enter eternity.'

When you can see that, as a human being, you are traveling on a timeline through your life. But that you are really eternity, a point of existence, travelling through time. You are a *time traveler*! So as eternal beings, many of us feel limited by time, confused by it. Rumi explains, 'You are the unconditioned spirit trapped in conditions, like the sun in eclipse'. The point of our time here is to understand that we can live in a conditioned state, of this plane, at this time, but without being limited by it. Anytime we feel limited by existence here, we can remember what it is to be *eternity*. We can change the ways in which we view time, and as we change our perception, we also change our relationship with it.

Love is the Bridge

Rumi said, 'Love is the bridge between you and everything'. As we apply our choices, we begin to live in and express the essence of our true selves. Establishing core boundaries and maintaining non-negotiable priorities are at the beginning of the journey towards alignment. Maslow's Hierarchy states that the basic tenants of existence include food, shelter, water, safety, and anything that the body needs to survive. Once we surpass survival, we step into choice and freedom, towards self-actualisation. Established and maintained boundaries provide space and structure for *more than* our needs, allowing us to explore our calling. We all strive to understand and reach a state of self-actualisation, and once the basics are provided for ourselves, it is possible to transcend surviving and evolve into thriving.

The transition to thriving involves finding deeper understanding of ourselves, and applying our greatest values, for ourselves and those around us. As we make choices that enhance our sense of happiness and wellbeing, we naturally begin to factor the wellbeing of others into the equation. For those of us who value a world with less suffering, we choose experiences that reduce the suffering within, through loving relationships, nurturing our bodies with healthy food, and activities that promote happiness. We also begin to see how our choices can do the same for others. We buy from companies with a high standard of ethics and integrity, who pay staff well, treat animals with respect, care for the planet, and have taken steps to reduce pollution. Our inner view becomes more worldly.

In this way, life becomes more simple, less complex. Each choice becomes easier to make, a more graceful application of our true values and priorities. Inner conflict is reduced with consistent application, as we feel more aligned with what we choose. This more worldly, inclusive view only comes as a result of understanding your priorities, which is necessary for a deeper understanding of how we connect, communicate, and interact with the world around us.

Chapter 17: Empathy for Evolution

We have all chosen to be here now, as human beings. Unfortunately, most of us struggle with what we believe to be a more difficult existence. Human emotions are complex, the body is complex, our interactions are complex, and we often feel overwhelmed by the experience. In order to learn, we begin to connect with others, to try to gain an understanding of human ideas and perspective. Empathic beings will all recognise the ways in which emotion has been overwhelming. Empathy is a quick and accurate way to assess the energy around us, to immediately know if a friend has a headache and needs to rest, or if a colleague is in a terrible mood and unable to cope with another difficulty. Empathy is a gift, and can provide clarity in any situation.

The problems begin when empathy causes confusion within ourselves. We feel the energy around us to gain clarity of what surrounds us, but this can cause confusion if we are unsure whether the energy is our own, potentially misinterpreting what we perceive.

I was an extremely sensitive empath as a child, which had a profound impact on my own development, my personality, and how I related with the world around me. I was always compassionate and caring. I would befriend the children that no one else wanted to play with, and always comforted other children in pain. I knew what others were experiencing, because I could feel it too. It became my role to try to ease the suffering and the pain, but doing so overwhelmed me. I grew exhausted with feeling the varying energies of the world around me, and processing it all through my empathic senses. As a response, I started to withdraw. Withdrawal is a protective measure, and because I was so sensitive, it became a way to survive. I withdrew physically and emotionally, never feeling comfortable enough to share space or connection with others. I was never a physically affectionate child, and still am not as an adult, which can be difficult for others to understand. But for those who are empathically sensitive, this is a protective measure, to maintain some clarity of energy and emotion.

When our emotions become overwhelming, or a source of confusion, the natural response is to try to dampen them down or push them away. We often develop coping strategies that can include anything from distracting ourselves with meaningless interactions, watching television, playing games online, to drinking, or using other substances to dull the sensation. The biggest problem with this response is that as we withdraw, or attempt to dull our experience, we pull away from our purpose. If our feelings guide us, but we choose to push them away, how are we to find the path? We attempt to protect ourselves from damage, but as we pull away from meaningful connection, we do the same within.

Traditional teachings state that we give and take energy, and that we feel most uncomfortable as we take on 'other people's stuff'. I used to believe this too, and while it helped me to imagine releasing another's energy as I set new boundaries, nothing fully resolved as a result. I believe that right now we can change the way we look at ourselves energetically, and revolutionise the healing process.

Most of us follow the model that states that life is an energetic exchange, a give and take. We give away our power, we take our mother's grief, we feel drained by those who are parasitical, or we surround ourselves with successful people so that we can feel elevated by the energy. But energy is energy, and it heeds intention. It will always flow towards equilibrium. Think of energy as a glass of water. We can pour water into one side of the cup, but it will even itself out, same as any other moveable substance. The energy wants to be in harmony, not a transaction or an exchange. As we seek to heal ourselves, we often feel broken, less than, damaged, and search for something to fill the hole within us. But this way of searching for resolution only perpetuates the belief that we are disconnected, or that we need to protect ourselves from the world around us.

Instead, we can see ourselves as fabric. A common technique for tie-dying a piece of fabric involves holding and twisting a chosen section. Once the fabric has been dyed, the twisting is released, producing a new colour, a new pattern. The fabric is not damaged, nothing is lost, it does not create a hole or rip. The process provides new colour, a unique pattern, all its own. Our experiences make us like that fabric. As we encounter situations that trigger us, the fabric of our energy is twisted, tightened. We are not broken; we do not lose a part of ourselves. There is simply a restriction in the flow as we focus upon what conflicts. As we learn from the experience, our outlook is coloured by each aspect.

Too many of us believe that we are broken or wounded. Impossible. We are indestructible and infinite. A careless statement, dismissal of our true nature, or directed abuse or anger cannot bend or break us. We must simply change our language, the ways we refer to ourselves and our lives. We act as though we are broken when we believe we are. Be like the fabric of life and let life colour your existence.

Chapter 18: Speaking to the Soul

As we learn to understand ourselves, we learn the language of energy, the language of *soul*. As we release old paradigms, old ways of thinking and being, the noise dies away. The world can often seem to be too loud, too much, too overpowering, but only when we hold the beliefs and emotion that no longer serves. As we release these by peeling away the labels and identities, we begin to hear the inner voice, the inner guidance, and return to ourselves.

Intuition, that soft voice within, is the greatest guide we could ever hope to find. And most of us have forgotten that voice, over years of listening to the logic, the fear, the voices of others. But the intuition is there, and we can learn to tune in, and turn it up: we are fluent in the language of intuition, once we decide to listen. Intuition is the small nudge to speak up, the flash of insight, the moment you 'hear' yourself saying what you really mean. Simple, subtle, and true.

The language of *soul* is very much the same. It is what guides our intuition, the gentle encouragement to speak up, to step up. The more we listen for the voice of intuition, the more we choose what aligns with our values, the more we begin to flow with the higher vibration of soul, and into our calling.

Everything Connects

There is so much information in the world, but a lot of it fails to cut to the core of the issue. We try to solve symptoms instead of the root cause of the problem. When I started working with clients, I began to identify and develop my strengths, my inner Sherlock Holmes. I have always been a keen observer, and able to find the connections in everything—because *everything* connects. A problem that manifests in the physical body always has an emotional component, although possibly seeming totally disconnected on the surface. There is always a cause and effect, and finding the cause allows resolution of an issue on multiple levels. As I began to engage my inner Sherlock, I began to see many of the same patterns, over and over again. What I found is that ultimately, any suffering, sadness, loss, or pain stems from a perceived disconnection with *soul*.

When I write about the soul, what I refer to is *our essence*, beyond the human body, eternal. As a soul, an incarnation of creation, we have the ability to live in this plane for a lifetime. Existing in this plane gives the illusion that we are separate from our soul, our source. The truth is that we *are* soul, not just a body. This feeling of separation creates the beliefs that we are lost, that we cannot access the truth of ourselves, and that we must live our lives feeling isolated, alone, alien. The response within many of us is to overcompensate, to try our best to conform: we feel alien, so we *must be* alien, and have a need to act and speak like a human being so that we will be accepted. We emulate the people closest to us, for better or worse, moving further away from our true selves. This allows us to immerse ourselves in the human experience. But we then spend our childhood and early years forgetting who we are, in order to conform, and then spend the rest of our lives rejecting what we have learned, to remember who we *are*.

Our calling, our soul purpose, is intertwined with our essence. As we learn to connect with one, we find the other. Often understanding your calling can lead you back to *you*.

Chapter 19: Remember Your Calling

Do you already know what your purpose is? Our purpose or calling is both the simplest and most complex part of existence, but only because we make it so. Each of us makes the courageous decision to join the ranks of human beings, to play a part, to make a difference. As a soul, we choose a calling for very specific reasons, for ourselves, and those around us. Most of us arrive, knowing exactly what we are meant to do, and then 'forgetting' over the course of a lifetime. We spend so much time and energy trying to be human, that we forget ourselves beyond these bodies, making it only natural to believe that we do not know our purpose, and fear that we will fail. The truth is that we are all living our calling, in this very moment.

Many of us believe that we are here for one grand moment, one massive event, and that if we do not change the entire world in a single act or statement, we will fail. This is because we forget the ripple effect: when a pebble is thrown into a still lake, the ripples in the water spread, and continue across the surface, many times farther than the size or reach of the tiny pebble. Our words and actions have the same ability, and our smallest interactions can have the largest effects. Do you know who Gandhi's teacher was? Or of the parents of the world's most influential leaders? You may have no awareness of them, but they will have shaped the thoughts and actions of the earth's most powerful beings. What if right now, you are teaching the next Oprah Winfrey, or parent to the next Deepak Chopra, or supportive friend to a future winner of the Nobel Peace

Prize? Often, our influence lies below the surface, the smaller ripples, but it is there nonetheless. Deepak Chopra wrote,'A body is what a particular swirl in a transpersonal flow of experiences looks like, just like a whirlpool is what a particular swirl in a stream of water looks like'. In this way, we are all connected to experience and consciousness, and so able to influence everyone around us. And so, we matter.

When it comes to our calling, it is important to look to the big *themes* spanning years or decades, as opposed to the shorter or smaller events. Look at the big picture of your life, your biggest roles and areas of influence. Are you a parent? Are you an artist or creator? Do you connect communities, or create forums for communication? Are you a healer? A teacher? Are you a catalyst for change? Do you have a caring capacity within yourself, where compassion is so natural, that you bring peace into every room you enter? Consider your identities over the course your life, the patterns that you see repeatedly over the years and decades. As you discover these incredible gifts and virtues, you will begin to see where they overlap, and where they will lead you.

When I look back at my life, at all of the choices that I made, either intentionally or not, I can see how I have been directed along my path. I was always a sensitive and compassionate child, and I cared for others who were not accepted. I studied Psychology at university, and for over a decade supported vulnerable people with very complex needs, those least accepted by society. All of this very obviously contributed to my calling as a healer or guide, a teacher, and a catalyst for change. I also waited tables, worked in a day care, a call centre, a clothing shop, and a school development office. All of these positions seem to be quite random, and the way I stumbled into some of them certainly was, but in every position I learned applicable skills and gained further clarity in my calling. Each of these roles taught me how to read people, to understand what makes them tick, and how to relate to others. I learned how to speak in a public setting, to be an advocate for others, and how to connect with humanity in a very deep and honest way. Although the roles were very different from each other on the surface, there were threads that connected them, common intentions, common ways of working.

If you are struggling to identify your calling, look to your past in order to find your future. If you feel that you are so off track that you cannot possibly be near it, you are closer than you think. When your life is so painful that you struggle to persevere, when you feel that you no longer know yourself, these are the breaking points for clarity. As you learn through the contrast of pulling against yourself, you begin to recognise the way back. For some, this is their calling: to lead the lost back to themselves, to bring them back home.

Serve the World, Don't Save it

You are the hero you have been waiting for, the hero, wizard, fairy godmother, the One. I once gave a talk on how choosing yourself would enable you to serve the world. The organiser thought I had meant *save* the world. In some ways she was right, but not in the way that most would assume. On some level, most of us believe that we have to save the world. We believe that if we do not fight to the death or sacrifice ourselves in a meaningful way, we will have failed. We fear the possibility of failing our mission, letting down all of humanity, and of suffering the consequences. But we are wrong. The ego will speak up at this point, reminding us that we have to continue to believe this. We want to believe that we are important and necessary. But this is simply a shallow reminder that we truly are.

You, as a luminous being, are not here to save the world. You are here to *serve* it. You will serve humanity in ways that are unique to you. You will find the gifts that are part of your calling and purpose, and you will succeed in having an impact. And through this, you will be relieved of the burden of saving anyone or anything. Because when we all serve the world, the world saves itself.

There is a huge difference between serving others and being a servant of obligation. Service is committed through acts of compassion, love, and sense of loyalty. Service is inspired action, not obligation. Those who serve choose it freely, and embody the best of themselves as they do. Our purpose is our own, but always involves others, and there will always be an element of service within living our purpose. We may paint a picture or write a song on our own, but it will touch the lives of dozens, hundreds, or thousands. Purpose will never separate you from human connection. It will help to connect us all.

Understanding how to serve freely allows us to find alignment, essence, the highest and best of who we are. By embracing freedom and releasing obligation, we live an authentic life, establish boundaries that honour purpose, and live from the inside out. And we begin to respond instead of react.

We all project our own thoughts and feelings, which are received by those around us. The less aware a person is of this, the more likely he or she is to simply react to what is being projected. This is evidenced by acting out of character, mood swings, and massive changes depending on the environment we are in, or company we keep. The clearer the boundaries, and the more spaciousness we have, the easier it is to remain centred and authentic. It becomes easier to consistently honestly speak from the heart, without confusion or outside influence. We can choose the ways in which we behave instead of simply reacting to another, showing an honest representation of who we really are. At that point, we have the ability to set the tone for our interactions, to influence the energy of the room, the quality of conversation, the level of vibration around us. And once we begin to apply this, we truly live in freedom.

As we begin to live a life of service, a service that we choose, we can release the belief that freedom is selfish. We can recognise that we are all here to serve others, and that by allowing ourselves to be free, and by choosing what contributes to our own happiness, we give others permission to be free and happy too. Choosing to feel good, to feel free, is not selfish or wrong. We talk about wanting peace in the world, we try to enforce peace in the world, but it does not work. As long as there is inner conflict within ourselves, it creates conflict in the world around us. If we all simply allow ourselves to be free, then there will be more freedom in the world. If we all allow ourselves to be peaceful, there will be more peace in the world. Whatever we allow feeds and amplifies the energy around us, and allows others to experience it too. Your peers can look to you and learn. Allowing yourself to live in alignment with truth, freedom, and love, is the most compassionate act you can commit, for yourself and the world.

Chapter 20: Your Barriers to Your Calling

Although each of us deeply desire to live our purpose, most of us are afraid to follow the path. It feels too big and too confusing that there is overwhelming pressure to get it right. We are terrified of failing, or of wasting an opportunity that will not be offered again.

We already know that our fears are the lies that we tell ourselves, the misalignment that we are currently living. We only fear a calling that we do not yet understand, or feel able to see the full picture. As a soul, you chose your callings, and you understand how they weave together, how they impact upon yourself, and the world around you. But all of the ways we delay or sabotage ourselves, are simply a way to avoid facing our fears. Marianne Williamson says, 'Our deepest fear is not that we are inadequate. Our deepest fear is that we are powerful beyond measure. It is our light, not our darkness that most frightens us. We ask ourselves, 'Who am I to be brilliant, gorgeous, talented, fabulous?' Actually, who are you not to be? You are a child of God. Your playing small does not serve the world. There is nothing enlightened about shrinking so that other people won't feel insecure around you. We are all meant to shine, as children do. We were born to make manifest the glory of God that is within us. It's not just in some of us; it's in everyone. And as we let our own light shine, we unconsciously give other people permission to do the same. As we are liberated from our own fear, our presence automatically liberates others'. We came here with purpose, of course we will be successful. Denying our purpose is the only thing that could possibly make our lives meaningless, but we could not truly ignore our calling, even if we tried.

Some of us are living our calling and do not know it. We may be afraid to be a leader, but we already are leading, in some capacity. We might be afraid to teach, but we are already teaching others, through example. If we are not immersed in our calling, we will be in the process of preparing ourselves for it—learning, practicing, readying ourselves in order to share. We often feel that we are wasting time, missing out, but we are actually preparing for the future and the divine calling that we have chosen. Allow yourself to live the process and enjoy it, because you cannot really get it wrong. You can distract yourself and delay, but inevitably, your calling is going to bring you back to your path, and guide you towards fulfilment.

What is your Archetype?

Our identities and labels may indicate a way into our calling. Although many labels may be outdated or misaligned, the most authentic can give an indication regarding specific archetypes, or roles that we embody. There is always an element of complexity to each label, depending upon experience and perception, and we can choose the aspects that we wish to express.

For example, consider the archetype of 'the Warrior'. The Warrior has a great sense of loyalty, honour, and purpose, and is able to see the 'bigger picture' of the family or community, and what best serves the group as a whole. Warriors are grounded in belief of what is right and what is wrong, and willingly defend what is precious. Warriors are willing to work towards a larger goal, despite time or effort expended in the duration. Warriors also have a tendency to sacrifice themselves for the good of others. While this may be a noble intention, if followed continuously, the Warrior risks living a lifetime of sacrificing happiness at the expense of others. Because of the Warrior's strong sense of right and wrong, patterns of conflict can be easily created, being quick to defend, possibly when there is no conflict to be had. Warriors will also often accept a life of hardship. In a world of abundance, this may not be necessary, and the Warrior may be wasting time or energy on difficulties, instead of creating a life that is aligned to purpose.

The reality is that there is nothing wrong with the Warrior archetype, or any other. If a person can find harmony within an archetype, and draw on the strengths, all can be powerful in creating a fulfilling existence. Deep healing and a sense of purpose can be found in re-channelling this energy. It is simply about finding another way to utilise it, to understand loyalty, community, to be inspired by compassion, love, and honour.

As we consider other archetypes, we can identify those which we align with, and the positive aspects that can apply. Other archetypes include the Hero, the Caregiver, the Romantic or Idealist, Explorer, Rebel, Creator, the Magician, the Teacher or Sage, Visionary, and Advocate. Consider the labels you give yourself, those that most resonate, and allow yourself to recognise the aspects that connect you with your higher self, and your path.

As we begin to understand our role in this world, our calling, we step into service, enabling us to find deep meaning for our own life and that of this world.

Chapter 21: Living Your Highest Potential

Do you avoid being the tallest poppy? When I was 10 years old, I won an art competition at school by drawing a picture for Earth Day, and I was so proud! I was awarded a t-shirt to wear on the school's parade through town. A passing woman saw my shirt and commented on it, and I happily exclaimed that I had won it. And one of my friends mocked me. This is the first time that I can remember being shamed for being happy, or for celebrating my success. Later, as I delved into the residual emotion and beliefs that this incident triggered, I began to recognise the subtle ways I have avoided sharing happiness and success in order to avoid a negative response from others. Many people struggle with issues around 'tall poppy syndrome', afraid to be seen as successful, powerful, or talented. In many cultures, we are taught to downplay our gifts, that we are not supposed to 'show off', that it is wrong boast or brag. But where do we draw the line between boasting and celebrating success, and what are the potential effects?

We all are here for various reasons, unique to each of us; we have things we want to accomplish, people we want to connect with, and to make an impact upon the world. But how can we do this if we hide our gifts? Our gifts are one of the best indicators of calling.

Gifts, talents, and passions guide us in the path towards accomplishing all that we are here to accomplish. Look back at your life, and remember the times that you hid your gifts, dulled yourself, dismissed your talents, or simply denied them. Remember the gifts and talents that you have denied, and imagine applying them now. For example, I know that I am not meant to be a famous artist, but I am meant to connect with others through open and honest expression. I know that when I deny this expression, I deny my divinity and the best of who I am. When we identify the greatest aspects of ourselves, the power, the love, the compassion, connection, expression, we allow these gifts to create our lives, and our world becomes an incredible place to inhabit.

Calling is something that we can begin to identify over time, through experience, recognising the ways that we are geniuses, the areas in which we thrive. Purpose lies where passion, talent, and dedication meet.

Passion is inspired from within; a deep love, that lights us up. Our passions can show us our priorities—what is necessary for a happy or fulfilling life. The pursuit of passion creates a sense of deep connection, within ourselves, which we can share with the world around us. Talent is something that we may be born with. We know others who find specific skill sets easy to master, who can apply little effort and succeed. When we engage our talents and strengths, we feel in our element, at home and totally confident within ourselves. The third element of dedication, or a choice to apply the other two, with focus, is what allows us to embody our passion and talent in a way that truly matters. A decision to live on purpose requires a sense of dedication to follow through.

I am passionate about music; I listen constantly, ask friends for recommendations, and transcend reality at live shows. I have enough passion to dedicate my life to music, but I do not have the talent. I practiced the piano for seven years, determined to improve, but I still struggle to learn a new piece of music. I have relatives who can hear a song and play it perfectly, by ear. They have both passion and raw talent, and dedication to pursue music through practice and performance. Not every talented, passionate artist is able to use their art to make a living, but they do use it to make their lives fuller, more complete. Creativity remains a regular part of their lives, because it is a part of expressing their essence. We need the combination of passion, talent, and dedication to find our calling and live it.

It is possible to be unaware of our gifts and talents, either because we were told to keep them to ourselves, or because we have not allowed ourselves to fully express them. Give yourself permission to express.

Mastery

Once we find our passions and talents, and the dedication to share them, we begin the journey to *mastery*. Mastery takes time, a bit of determination, and a willingness to devote energy to growth. One of my favourite examples of mastery is the way that Prince created and shared his music. During his concerts, every note was pitch perfect, and every moment was beautifully choreographed. He surrounded himself with the most incredible musicians, passionate, and masters of their art. Prince invested the time, dedication, blood, sweat, and tears to *embody* music, no separation between him and his craft.

I have always deeply appreciated those who immerse themselves. The subject or focus is of less importance, I simply appreciate an opportunity to engage with a person who has delved into an art, a philosophy, a craft, and is willing to share it with the world. There is often pressure in the world to be good at everything: the best parent, boss, employee, driver, speaker, designer, cook. The pursuit of unachievable perfection is both exhausting and shallow. Mastery comes to a person who has tapped into his passion, found her faith, resonated with purpose and has taken the plunge.

In which areas are you already a master, or developing your mastery? What are you always hungry to know more about, be around, hear, feel, read, consume? If you have not yet found your mastery, there could be some avoidance at play. Most of us are good at beginning a project, and completing ninety percent of it. But that final ten percent is the hardest part; it takes the most focus and detail. The ten percent is where we become masters. Most fail to reach the final ten percent. We quit before the full immersion and move onto something easier, with less depth, with less commitment, taking the easy way out. That final ten percent is what produces the greatest artwork, most beautiful compositions, most graceful expression possible. How are you willing to commit to that final ten percent? What are you ready to master?

The mastery that we commit to can expand our perception of what is possible. There is a lot of emphasis on potential. We touch our highest potential as we step into mastery, and come the closest that we possibly can to living our *divinity*. Before we reach this state, we begin to identify what limits us, what stops us from reaching our highest potential. Most of this stems from comparison—a feeling that we cannot reach the same height as someone else.

Who inspires you? And what is stopping you from *becoming* that inspiration? It can be easy to feel a little star struck by our heroes, mentors, and leaders. But they are people too. Everyone whom we look up to has made mistakes, has failed many times, has had to find his or her way. Once we understand that they had to transcend the drama, conflict, distraction of daily human life, then we realise that the rest of us can too. We all have the potential to live, learn and grow. We all have the capacity to become more than what we project, in the present moment.

So if you have the same potential as everyone else, what is holding you back? What is stopping you from being the very best you can be, at what you do? What keeps you from embodying your gifts, passions, and talents, and applying them in your daily life? What are you waiting for? Allow yourself to dream your biggest dreams. What is it that you truly want for your life, without settling, without compromising?

When you consider your highest potential, focus on the things that get in the way. What takes up time, energy, and focus, that does not contribute to you living your best life? What are your biggest distractions? And why are you allowing them any part of your life? Understand exactly what you want for yourself, and identify what you can let go of that will create space to allow it. As you release your resistance to living your potential, you give yourself permission to become the highest version of yourself. Stop being passive, take a stand. To witness miracles you have to do something out of place. Disrupt your own life, your thoughts, your patterns, and become a greater version of you.

Chapter 22: Final Thoughts

There is a big difference between thinking, believing, planning, and actually doing. There is a big difference between establishing boundaries and actually living them. Because we are physical beings, there is a physical element to everything. We can wish and hope to become a millionaire, and it may miraculously happen, but at the very least we could buy a lottery ticket. We have to help the universe out, and meet it halfway. There has to be a physical action to go along with beliefs and intention. The clearer our belief systems are, the more we believe and feel what we want, the easier it is to manifest. But living is really about stepping in and recognising when action will support the intention.

Whatever you can do that helps you understand yourself more, of who you really are on a *soul* level, will be useful and worthwhile. Understanding comes from experience, by trying something new. Often we say we want change, but are actually doing nothing to facilitate it. We want our businesses to grow, dynamics to evolve, to have more fun, but are not taking any steps to create. The more we actively engage with life, the more we get from it. The more we understand what aligns, the more we step into the essence of what makes the soul sing and feel amazing. The more authentic, honest, and truthful we are, the more synchronicity and serendipity is experienced, simplifying life, releasing the drama, providing clarity. The moments of synchronicity, where events just click into place, are the greatest moments in life. The more you live your calling and follow your purpose, the more common these moments will be. Imagine a life that is full of little miracles, every day.

We have infinite number of choices and opportunities each day. The growth comes with an understanding of our choices, and the impact, the ripple effect that they will have. What we choose on a daily basis is what is creating our world. The conversations that we choose to have, or not to have, every word or action chosen has an impact. It ultimately comes back to choosing how we want to feel, what we want to do, what we are here to align with and create within this lifetime. The little decisions matter, because they indicate what is happening on deeper levels within. Self-sabotage and denial can be very subtle. Allow yourself to start, to begin. You are afraid because you do not know where the start will lead. But you will not gain clarity until you begin. Do not listen to your fears, listen to the truth, listen to your heart. Pay attention to what feels good. Get into the habit of tuning into your body and choosing what feels light, what feel expansive, what feels fun or exciting or nurturing. Listen to that. We pay too much attention to fear. Find the goodness, and follow that, absolutely. Keep taking the time to connect with the energy of soul and essence and get your answers from there. If we are avoiding conversations, being seen, being heard, all we are doing is delaying. We are avoiding living our calling. We are actually delaying our own sense of well-being, health, and happiness. If you discover that you are delaying or avoiding, then deal with it today. Identify what changes you can make, what decisions you can make, and invite some grace into your life. Whether the issue is your health, relationships, or work, see what you can do to change the dynamics. Remember to look at what you are avoiding, because that will always be your biggest step in evolution. When you face what you are avoiding, you face yourself, and this will always make the biggest difference in your *being*.

As you allow yourself to move beyond your comfort zone, you move into the cutting edge of life. Existence is infinitely more vibrant and colourful there.

About the Author

Jennifer Main is writer and a transformational guide. Her background in Psychology, and experience working with beautifully complex beings from all walks of life, have facilitated her role as a leading instructor of health and wellbeing in the United Kingdom, as well as an international speaker and instructor.

Jennifer was awarded a BSc in Psychology in 2001 and worked with young offenders, and adults with complex needs for over a decade in the USA and UK. She began to delve more into healing and philosophy in 2008, and soon became one of the leading instructors in the United Kingdom. Over the past 20 years, she has dedicated her time and energy to understanding the subconscious, identity, manifesting, creation, consciousness, quantum mechanics, and all aspects of soul purpose and embodiment.

Her website, JenniferMain.co.uk, is a haven, meant to bridge the gap between the etheric and the physical for exploration, creativity and expression, consciousness, soul alignment, grounded spirituality, magic and miracles, science and study, and truth. You are very welcome to join her tribe!

Made in the USA
Columbia, SC
19 May 2017